How To Raise Your Kids in Troubled Times

by

Buddy and Pat Harrison

Harrison House
Tulsa, Oklahoma

*How To Raise Your Kids in Troubled Time*s
ISBN 0-89274-635-1
Copyright © 1993 by Buddy and Pat Harrison
P. O. Box 35443
Tulsa, Oklahoma 74153

Published by Harrison House, Inc.
P. O. Box 35035
Tulsa, Oklahoma 74153

Contents

Introduction

The home is very important to God. In fact, He created families before He created the Church. When God created Adam and Eve, He placed them in relation to each other and to their children. He established the family as the pattern for all mankind because He wanted us to live together as families.

God never intended for us to be isolated and independent beings, running around doing our own thing. He created us to live together — husband, wife and children — so we could love and care for each other.

The family is important because it helps us understand God as our heavenly Father. Because we love and care for our children, we can better understand God's great love and care for us. To be better parents, we can look to Him as our example. We can more easily understand our children's struggles when we consider our own struggles as God's children.

A true Christian home is one of the greatest witnesses of the Gospel to our sin-sick world. People watch how we live. They hear what we *do* much louder than what we *say*. That's why a family committed to God has tremendous influence on the world. A family that follows the divine leadership of the Lord Jesus Christ is a living, breathing demonstration of the love of God, the power of the Holy Spirit and the abundant life that is available to believers.

A Christian home is a tremendous witness because it exists where people live. It exists in the nitty-gritty of life where people laugh and cry and love. The Church is important, but the Christian home is the heart and life of the Church.

Being a Christian parent is probably the most important and challenging job you can take on today. It is rewarding, exasperating, joyful and sometimes overwhelming. You can laugh, cry, love and pray more than you ever thought possible.

So much depends on how well we raise our kids to love and serve the Lord Jesus Christ. More is at stake than their individual lives or even the well-being of our families. The very future of the Church, the Body of Christ, rests on how well we do our job as Christian parents.

The message of the Gospel won't go forth if we don't train up our young people to carry on the work of Jesus Christ. Not only are we to teach our kids the Word of God, we should also let them see the power of the Holy Spirit in action. Otherwise, the Church will someday have only a form of godliness which denies the power thereof. (2 Tim. 3:5.)

The Bible has much to say about Christian parenting. One of its best verses is not very well-known: **We will tell the next generation the praiseworthy deeds of the Lord, his power, and the wonders he has done** (Ps. 78:4 NIV).

The future of our nation rests with our children. Today, as never before, we are seeing an all-out assault on the hearts, minds and souls of our kids. Satan is using every temptation possible to snare them. He knows that by destroying them, he can destroy the home. By destroying the Christian home, he can destroy America. If we lose our children to him, we as a nation will be defeated. While we struggle with the evil in the world, we can be defeated from within, and our defeat could come more quickly and completely than we ever thought possible.

That's why in recent years we have become more and more concerned about children. We are deeply concerned about the tremendous task that Christian parents face today in raising their kids for Jesus Christ. We are struggling with forces and issues that no other generation has had to deal with.

And while the problems have increased, it seems that the availability of clear-cut Bible answers has decreased. Everywhere we turn there seems to be another self-proclaimed "child expert" telling us how to raise our kids, how to deal with our problems, what everything means and what to do when it happens. But few are providing us with real answers based on the Word of God and faith in Him.

Parents are hurting today. Many are confused and afraid. They need sound biblical answers to the problems facing them. This is why we wanted to share with you what we have learned through the years from the Scripture as well as from the experiences we have had raising our own children. What knowledge we have on this subject is partially from doing what we knew was right, but a great deal was learned from what we did wrong. We want to pass along to you what we have learned from our mistakes as well as our successes. And we also want to pass along what we have learned from studying as many other parents as we could whom we saw raise their children to love and serve the Lord Jesus Christ and to carry on His work.

We certainly don't claim to have all the answers, but there are some basic principles and suggestions that can help to guide you through difficult days. We haven't dealt with every situation that Christian parents face, but we have tried to include the important issues that you may have to deal with. And we have tried to be as candid and practical as possible. You don't need some pie-in-the-sky theological answer. You need practical, down-to-earth wisdom from the Word of God.

One of the most important truths we can share with you is this: God is on your side and He will never — NEVER — fail you.

Maybe your situation seems impossible. Maybe you are tired. Maybe your wisdom and experience are exhausted. But God is there to help you. Remember, He will never leave you nor forsake you. (Heb. 13:5.) He wants you to succeed even more than you want to succeed.

He will give you the strength and wisdom — and even the endurance — you need to help you through whatever comes your way. You may be facing a bad situation, but He will always help you go through it with power and victory.

The second truth we want to remind you of is this: God doesn't require you to be a perfect parent raising perfect children. He only asks that you yield yourself to Him and give Him your best. Then He will provide His grace, His love and His patience to help you. He will give you the Holy Spirit to guide you, to live in you and through you, to help you be like Him in spite of your human ways.

Remember, you were a sinner, but you have been saved by grace — and so has your child if he has accepted Jesus Christ. But no matter how hard you try or how much you may want it to be, you will never be perfect in this earthly life. And neither will your child. Sometimes we put ourselves under condemnation because we make mistakes. And we don't let our children be human and make mistakes either.

The home is, after all, the place where we live out God's grace. It's the testing ground of faith. It's the place where we can struggle and fail and begin again, where we forgive and are forgiven, where we love and are loved without reservation. It should be a place where we can laugh together and enjoy each other.

It's our prayer that this book will help you to raise your children in the admonition of the Lord. (Eph. 6:4.)

The Lord never intended for Christian parenting to be a totally overwhelming task. We believe His Word contains the answers you need, and the Holy Spirit has the power you need to do your job well. He's willing and ready to help you, because He knows that what you do as a parent is vitally important to your child...to our nation...and to the kingdom of God.

1

The Importance of a Parent's Faith

Many parents today could say to us: "Buddy and Pat, the world is in terrible shape. Sin is on the rampage. How can I compete with its influence on my kids? How can I raise them to serve Jesus Christ?"

If that's your desire, too, there are two important ways we might respond to you.

Know Jesus Christ Personally

It is vitally important that you really know Jesus Christ personally as your Lord and Savior, and that you are living for and serving Him. You can't very well raise your kids to serve the Lord if you don't serve Him, too.

One minister we know was sitting around with friends back during his Bible school days. They were all taking turns telling about their personal experience with the Lord. When they got to the last fellow, he just said, "Oh, I was always saved; I was born in a Christian home."

Maybe you too were born in a Christian home, but that won't make anybody a Christian. No matter where you were born, you were born into sin. It makes no difference how good your mom and dad may have been; you were still born into sin. There comes a time in your life when you have to repent of your sins and say, "Lord, I'm a sinner, so please forgive me." You have to experience salvation for yourself.

God has no grandchildren — only sons and daughters! It doesn't matter if you were baptized as an infant or if you went to church every time the doors were open. You may have looked like a Christian and acted like one. You may have attended church and Sunday school all your life, and you may know the Bible inside out. But you can never really experience God's presence in your heart until you have confessed your sins and accepted His forgiveness.

You have to accept Jesus Christ as your personal Lord and Savior before you can be a true Christian, a born-again child of God. You have to pray a simple prayer like this:

Jesus, I don't know You, but I want to. The Bible says You died on the cross to save sinners. Lord, I'm a sinner, so I ask You to forgive my sins and put Your Holy Spirit in me to help me live as You want me to live.

Thank You, Lord, for Your forgiveness and for making me a brand-new person.

A little prayer like that — if you prayed it with a sincere heart and meant every word of it — opens the gates of heaven for you. Second Corinthians 5:17 says, **Therefore if any man be in Christ, he is a new creature: old things are passed away; behold, all things are become new.** Jesus said, **I am the way, the truth, and the life: no man cometh unto the Father, but by me** (John 14:6).

If you really want to raise your children to serve the Lord, the first thing you have to do is serve Him yourself.

Have Faith in God Like Moses' Parents

A second thing we can do when parents ask how they can raise their kids for Jesus Christ is to point them to the story of Moses.

Moses stood against the most powerful man of his time, Pharaoh — and he won! He led over three million people out of bondage in Egypt. He took them across the Red Sea, guided them through 40 years of wandering in the wilderness, and led them to the Promised Land.

But, you know, the real heroes of that story are Moses' parents. If it hadn't been for them, Moses probably would never have served God. In fact, if it hadn't been for their faith in God, Moses would have been killed as an infant.

Times are tough these days, but they weren't exactly a picnic in Moses' day either. The book of Exodus, chapters 1 and 2, tell us how the children of Israel were slaves in Egypt. They knew only hard work as they toiled for their Egyptian taskmasters. Then things got even worse!

Pharaoh heard rumors that God was going to raise up a deliverer to set His people free. So to keep this from happening, he ordered that all male Hebrew babies be put to death at birth.

Can you imagine the horror and fear each Hebrew woman must have felt when she realized she was pregnant, and then gave birth to a baby boy?

Well, right in the middle of all that, the Baby Moses was born. By law, his parents were supposed to throw him in the river and let him drown. But Moses had parents who weren't afraid of Pharaoh. They had faith in God, so they hid their baby for three months.

> **By faith Moses, when he was born, was hid three months of his parents, because they saw he was a proper [NIV: no ordinary] child; and they were not afraid of the king's commandment.**
>
> **Hebrews 11:23**

Moses' parents saw that he was no ordinary baby, so they trusted God. They had enough faith to stand against Pharaoh. Faith like that in parents will be passed on to their children. Your kids know whether or not you believe and trust God. Because Moses' parents had faith, it was bred into his life.

By the time Moses was three months old, it was getting difficult for his parents to hide him. They knew they would have to do something. That's when his mother got an inspiration from God. She made a little homemade boat — a basket — and put her baby into it. Then she pushed that basket out into the Nile River.

She knew she couldn't take care of her baby any longer. He was getting so big that she couldn't hide him. So she took the responsibility for him out of her own hands and put it into the hands of God. She had done all she could, so she had to let go of her child.

This is a message for every parent today: for you to have peace about looking out for your kids, put them in God's hands! You can't watch them every minute of the day, so you have to learn to commit them to God.

This is what a dedication service at church is all about. When your pastor dedicates your baby, you are acknowledging that your child is a gift from God. And you are putting that precious gift back into God's hands for His care and protection.

Once you have done that, you don't have to worry about your kids anymore. If you are living in obedience to God, Satan's power can't defeat them because the blessing of God is on them for the rest of their lives. God knows how to take care of them because you have committed them into His trust!

We Have To Do What We Can

Now, this doesn't mean that when your child is born, you can just turn him over to God with the attitude: "Well, here he is, God. He's Yours, so now You raise him." No, we have to do what we can. Then we let God do what He can. Just as you feed and clothe in the natural, you must do the same in the spiritual.

God has put that child in your hands to raise him the very best you know how. And He has given gifts to you as a parent which you are to use in raising him. Many times we have thoughts and feelings that we call "intuition" or "instinct," but really they come from God.

Moses' mother did something that didn't make sense in the natural: she put her infant son in a basket and pushed it out into the river. But the Lord was at work there. He inspired her plan and planted that thought in her mind. She didn't have a pastor she could go to for advice. She had to use what she had: a love of God, faith that He would help her, her own instincts and wisdom as a mother and her unselfish love for her son.

Sometimes when we need God's help with our kids, we look around for some supernatural manifestation of God in their lives. At times, He does act supernaturally; but, most of the time, He acts through us as the parents. He gives us ideas. He guides our decisions. He gives us wisdom and a knowing about what is best for our children.

While our children are in our hands, God expects us to use the resources He has given us to raise them for Him. When human logic and ability fail, we have the assurance that He will help us. And when the time comes to turn them loose, we still have the promise that He will never leave them. It's God and us working together.

Now, that doesn't mean we will never make a mistake. It means that even when we do, God can and will turn it into something good. Our kids can forgive us our mistakes if they know that we love them unconditionally, that we are committed to them and to God and that we are doing the best we can.

Discover God's Plan for Your Children

When Moses' mother pushed him out onto the water, the Holy Spirit immediately took control and started steering that basket on its way. She had done all she could for her son. From then on, it was up to God.

As a parent, when you come to the end of your human abilities and wisdom, you can steer your children into God's hands. Then you can let go, knowing beyond a shadow of a doubt that God is in control, and your children won't be tossed by every wave that comes along. The Holy Spirit will still be there to lead, guide and discipline those youngsters.

When we put our kids into God's hands, He always does a better job than we ever could. Moses' parents tried to protect their son and hide him from Pharaoh. But when God took over the situation, He dropped their baby right into Pharaoh's lap! He did just the opposite of what the parents would have done.

Isaiah 55:9 tells us that God's ways are higher than our ways and His thoughts are higher than our thoughts. When we have a problem with our kids, we are tempted to pray, "Now, God, You need to do such-and-such." But we often make decisions directly opposite from the way God wants it done.

We have to learn to turn our children over to God and let Him guide their lives. We have to realize that it's not our battle anymore — it's God's. And He knows how to take care of our kids much better than we do. As long as we keep trying to run the show, we will only get everything all fouled up. When God says, "Let Me handle it," then things will start to come together.

It's so important that we as parents be aware of God's purposes for our children. Most of us have dreams for them, and we try to direct them in certain ways — and there is nothing wrong with that — but if we aren't careful, we will let our own desires for them win out over God's. We have to remember that God has a will, a plan and a purpose for every child's life, and we need to seek Him to understand what His will, plan and purpose are.

We need to teach our children that they each have definite gifts and callings on their lives. We need to nurture and support and develop those gifts and callings so they will grow up, not to be what we think is important, but to fulfill God's will and plan for their lives.

Proverbs 22:6 in *The Amplified Bible* says, **Train up a child in the way he should go [and in keeping with his individual gift or bent], and when he is old he will not depart from it.**

There Are No Coincidences With God — He Is Never Surprised!

"It was a coincidence!" That's what the world says it was when Baby Moses floated down by Pharaoh's house where his daughter was bathing. Just a coincidence! But there are no coincidences to the child of God. The Lord is in control. There are no chances. God isn't going to turn you or your children over to chance.

Now, there are those who would say Pharaoh's daughter just happened to be out in the river bathing when Moses' little basket floated by. Then — as they say — just by chance, at that very moment, Moses got hungry and let out a cry!

But do you see how God was working out His plan? Moses' cries got the attention of Pharaoh's daughter. When she saw that baby, she fell in love with him. Everyone loves a baby, regardless of its color — red, yellow, brown, black or white. A baby is a baby.

Pharaoh's daughter picked up little Moses and took him right inside the house to the very man who wanted him dead! See how God works? Now, we wouldn't have done that, but God was handling the situation.

Pharaoh wanted all the Hebrew baby boys killed, but God said: "I'll fix Pharaoh! He wants to kill this Hebrew baby, but I'll have him raise this child. I'll have him buy the milk and supply all the clothing this baby needs. Moses will be raised right in Pharaoh's house, right under his nose!"

You see, when you let God take the responsibility for your kids, He might not do things the way you would — but He will do them better! It takes a lot of faith to keep trusting God when it looks like things are going in the opposite direction. And it takes a lot of faith to raise your kids God's way in today's world.

Pharaoh's daughter knew nothing about raising a baby, so she started looking around for help. And who do you suppose was waiting in the wings? Moses' mother! Another "coincidence." So Pharaoh's daughter said to her, **Take this child away, and nurse it for me, and I will give thee thy wages** (Ex. 2:9).

Now picture Moses' mother thinking something like this: "Thank You, God, for taking care of my baby! I could never provide for him the way You are!"

This is a God Who knows how to take care of everything you commit into His hands — and He will bless you while He's doing it!

While all the other Hebrew mothers lost their baby boys, Moses' mother was able to take care of him — and Pharaoh was paying her to do it! She was given the opportunity not only to raise her son but also to teach him about God. First, she gave him to God; then God gave him back to her, so she could teach him during the most important formative years of his life. That's the kind of God we serve!

Making a Difference in Your Child's Life

Moses grew up with the best of everything. He grew up in Pharaoh's house as the son of Pharaoh's daughter. He went to the finest schools and wore the finest clothes. He had everything he wanted — and then some. As far as the world was concerned, Moses had it made!

It would have been so easy for him to turn his back on his family and his people. After all, they were only slaves. Who could blame him for choosing the rich, easy life as Pharaoh's grandson? But those early years of teaching and training by his mother stuck with him. He had his parents' faith in him, and when it came time for him to choose, he chose God.

> **By faith Moses, when he was come to years, refused to be called the son of Pharaoh's daughter;**
> **Choosing rather to suffer affliction with the people of God, than to enjoy the pleasures of sin for a season;**
> **Esteeming the reproach of Christ greater riches than the treasures in Egypt: for he had respect unto the recompence of the reward.**
> **Hebrews 11:24-26**

Never underestimate your influence as a parent. You play the central role in the development of your kids, and you can make a difference in their lives.

Sure, drugs and sex and perversion are everywhere.

Sure, peer pressure is a strong force against Christian values and morals.

But the Bible says, **...greater is he that is in you, than he that is in the world** (1 John 4:4).

You can affect the lives of your children for Jesus Christ. You can teach and train them so that when it comes time for them to choose for themselves, they will choose God.

2

Your Prayers
Will Make a Difference

Being a Christian parent is hard work. It's blood, sweat and tears. But, praise God, He has given you some powerful weapons to help you be victorious in raising your children for Him.

One of the most important things you can do for your kids is to pray for them.

Now, we aren't talking about some little prayer that you memorize and recite once in a while. We are talking about spending time daily in prayer with your heavenly Father — a time when you press in and ask God to set a hedge around your children and keep them from the Enemy.

Someday one of your kids — whether son or daughter — may run from you. He may run away from the Church. He may run from living according to God's Word. But always remember this: he can never run away from God.

> Whither shall I go from thy spirit? or whither shall I flee from thy presence?
>
> If I ascend up into heaven, thou art there: if I make my bed in hell, behold, thou art there.
>
> If I take the wings of the morning, and dwell in the uttermost parts of the sea;
>
> Even there shall thy hand lead me, and thy right hand shall hold me.
>
> If I say, Surely the darkness shall cover me; even the night shall be light about me.

Yea, the darkness hideth not from thee; but the night shineth as the day: the darkness and the light are both alike to thee.

Psalm 139:7-12

Remember, your child can't get away from your prayers.

In Matthew 15:22-28 we find the story of the Canaanite woman whose daughter had a demon. The woman came to Jesus and begged Him to deliver her child from the demon. Now, it wasn't the daughter who came to Him for help. Maybe she couldn't come, or wouldn't. For whatever reason, it was the mother who came, and she was determined to get help. She cried out to Him, pleading for Him to help her daughter, for as a Canaanite she had no covenant right, but she had great faith.

His disciples didn't like the way she was crying out to Him, so they said: "Lord, make this woman leave us alone. She's following us around, crying and making a scene. You've got to do something!"

But Jesus said, **I am not sent but unto the lost sheep of the house of Israel...It is not meet to take the children's bread, and to cast it to dogs** (vv. 24,26). He was saying to her: "I've been sent to help the Jews, and you're not a Jew. You're a Gentile. The Jews think of you Gentiles as dogs. It isn't right to take the children's food and throw it to the dogs."

Now if He said those things to some of us today, we might get a little huffy and say, "How dare that preacher call me a dog! If He doesn't want to help me, I'll just go somewhere else. The nerve of that guy! He probably couldn't help my daughter anyway!"

But that little mother knew Jesus was her only hope. She had already put aside her pride. She didn't care what Jesus called her as long as He helped her daughter, so she said: **Truth, Lord: yet the dogs eat of the crumbs which fall**

from their masters' table (v. 27). In other words, she was saying, "Lord, just give me a crumb. That's all I need, because even a little of Your mercy is enough to help my daughter."

Persevering Prayer Moves the Heart of God

Talk about faith and perseverance! *That's the kind of prayer that moves the hand of God.*

Then Jesus said to her, **O woman, great is thy faith: be it unto thee even as thou wilt** (v. 28). And her daughter was set free from Satan at that very moment!

Do you want your child set free from Satan's influence? Are you willing to put aside your pride, get on your face before God, and pray until He answers? That's what it will take. You have to be willing to pray for your child every day, every week, every year until he (or she) is rooted and grounded in Jesus Christ.

You may say, "I've been praying for my child for years, but he's still living for the devil. What should I do?"

Or maybe you say, "I wasn't a Christian when my kids were small, so I didn't raise them to serve God. What can I do now that they're grown?"

Just keep praying for them. The final tally isn't in. As long as your children are still living, you keep praying. God will honor your prayers. We believe strongly in the power of prayer, so pray for them and claim them for God.

Ask God to build a wall of protection around them and keep them from every kind of harm: sin, sickness, disease, infirmity, drug addiction, alcohol, accidents, perversion, any plague that might come nigh their dwelling. (Ps. 91:10.) That covers every force that can come against a child physically, mentally, emotionally and spiritually.

And, you know, because of your prayers, one of these days your son or daughter may come directly to you and say something like this: "I accepted Jesus because you prayed for me. You claimed me for God and put God's mark on me. You rebuked Satan in my behalf, and I'm here today because you did. I thank God for you, for your love, and for your prayers."

Moses became a great man, but the roots of his greatness went back to when he was a child. He had parents who instilled the faith of God in his heart.

Many of the young children in churches today come from parents who believe God and pray for them. These are their roots. One young man, after being healed of polio, said, "I had a praying mama!" And one young lady said, "My grandmother held me before God!" Isn't that beautiful?

Don't give up on your children. As long as they have breath, there is hope. So claim them for God!

Start Praying Today

Don't wait until trouble comes. Start now to undergird your children with the strong power of prayer. No matter how young or how old they are, they will benefit from your prayers.

First of all, pray for your children's salvation. Then pray concerning the things they have to face in life — not just the big things, but the little, day-by-day things that come up before them.

Pray for God's purpose and plan for each of your children, in the present and the future: *What kind of job will he someday hold? Who will she marry? What kind of person does God want him to be?*

And while you are praying for them, pray for yourself. Pray each day that God will help you be the kind of parent you need to be. Pray for His wisdom and guidance in working out the practical, day-to-day realities of child rearing.

If God only wanted us to be saved, He could strike us dead as soon as we accepted Him. But the truth is, He wants us to be victorious in this life as well as the next. As a parent, you have the greatest opportunity to help your kids live victorious lives, through both your prayers and your example.

How blessed are the children whose mother and/or father know how to pray! They will never be able to escape the power of those prayers.

Example of Prayer for Your Children

Father, in Jesus' name, we pray for our children, surrounding them with our faith in You as our Lord and faith in Your Word, knowing that You watch over Your Word to perform it.

We believe, Lord, that our children are Your disciples, taught by You and obedient to Your will. We believe that great is their peace and undisturbed composure. We believe that You, Father, contend with that which contends with them, and You give them safety and ease them.

Father, we believe You will perfect that which concerns us, and we cast the care of our children, once and for all, over on You.

We confess that our children obey us, their parents, in the Lord. They honor, esteem and value us as precious to them, for this is the first commandment with a promise: that all may be well with them and that they may live long on the earth.

As their parents, we will train them in the way they should go, and when they are old they will not depart from it.

Our children are the head and not the tail. They shall be above only, and they shall not be beneath. They are blessed when they come in and go out.

We pray that our children will choose life, because they love You, Lord; that they will obey Your voice and cling to You, for You are their life and the length of their days.

We believe that You give Your angels charge over them to accompany them, defend them, and preserve them in all their ways. You are their refuge and their fortress.

Now we thank You, Lord, for hearing our prayer and our confession of faith. We give You all the praise and honor as the God Who is more than enough!

Scripture References

Jeremiah 1:12	Deuteronomy 30:19,20
Isaiah 54:13; 49:25	Deuteronomy 28:6,13
1 Peter 5:7	Psalm 91:2,11
Psalm 138:8	Proverbs 22:6

3
Show Your Children Who God Is

In an airport one day, a couple with their little girl was waiting for the grandparents to get off the plane. When a white-haired couple came down the ramp, the little girl started shouting, "Grandma! Grandpa!" Then she ran up to them, hugging and kissing them.

While waiting for the luggage, a man started chatting with the parents. He said, "I noticed how much your little girl loves her grandparents. They must visit you often."

"Oh, no," said the mother. "In fact, this is their first visit since our daughter was a baby."

"Then how did she recognize them? How could she know someone she hasn't seen?"

"Oh, we've been showing her pictures of Grandma and Grandpa almost every day, and we talk about them all the time."

No wonder she feels like she knows them.

You Are Your Children's Picture of God

After praying for your children, the most important thing you can do for them is to show them Who God is and make Him so real to them that they can know Him.

You may ask, "How can I show my kids what God is like? I don't have a picture of Him on my wall so they can see Him."

You are your children's picture of God. When they look at you, study you and watch you, they see what God is like.

A child's mind can't grasp the immensity of a God he can't see. But he can relate to God through his daddy who plays with him and through his mother who cares for him.

As a parent, you control your children's world. To them, you are all powerful. In their childish mind, you are like God and God is like you.

If you are loving and forgiving, your children see God as a loving and forgiving heavenly Father.

If you value your children and see them as individuals of dignity and worth, they will feel that they are also of worth to God.

If you discipline your children and expect them to obey you, they will see God as a figure of authority Who also expects their obedience.

This principle is especially true for fathers. Because God is our heavenly Father, we interpret Who God is by what our earthly fathers are like. So, Dad, the way you are is the way your children think God is.

One young man in New York City was being raised only by his mother. Whenever he heard his pastor talk about praying to our heavenly Father and loving Him, he couldn't relate. His own father had beaten him, used drugs and abandoned him and his mother.

Then one night that boy dreamed about God. He said, "In my dream, God told me He was my Father. He told me He loved me and wanted to take care of me and help me. Now I know Who my heavenly Father really is!"

None of us can always be a perfect parent. But if we can show love and forgiveness — if we can use our God-given authority in a loving and caring way — our kids will be better able to understand God's love, forgiveness and authority.

Too many of us have grown up feeling like we had to perform for our parents in order to be loved. We had to get good grades, clean up our rooms, or do what they told us to do in order for them to love us. And when we didn't measure up — when we were "bad" — we felt like they didn't love us.

We often have that same image of God. When we are "good people" and go to church, we feel good about God and His attitude toward us. But when we have sinned, when we have disobeyed God, we tend to withdraw from Him. We don't pray as much or read our Bible. We stay out of church because we don't see how God could love us as much.

But God loves us no matter what — whether we are good or bad!

Look at Israel. In the Old Testament they were always chasing after other gods. In one breath, God was correcting them; and in the next breath, He was loving them back to Himself. No matter what they did — or did not do — He never stopped loving them. And that's the kind of parent we should be.

God has given us the responsibility to be His representative to our children. The way we live and act and react reflects Him. This is one of the reasons God created the home, because there is no better place for a child to learn the nature of God and his great value to God than at home. And there are no better teachers than his own parents.

Set a Godly Example

Now, don't get us wrong. We don't want to put some heavy burden on you by saying you have to be perfect or your children will reject God. No one is perfect. And you will never be perfect — at least, not in this life. What matters is how you live over the long haul.

Yes, you will make mistakes because you are human. In fact, the way you act when you make a mistake, when you sin, can teach your kids positive things about God.

When you sin, do you come to God, humble and broken? Do you acknowledge that what you did was wrong and that you are accountable to God and under His authority? Do you get on your face before Him asking forgiveness for what you have done, and then accept His forgiveness?

If you do, then you are showing your children the truth: that you truly are God's child, and no matter what you may do, He will always love you. You are telling them that it's okay to make mistakes if you are man or woman enough to admit it and ask forgiveness.

You will make mistakes as a parent — we all do. The important thing is how you present yourself to your kids. Are you loving, forgiving, merciful and fair? Do you discipline and exercise authority in love? Do you forgive and forget? Are you patient, kind, humble? Do you bear all things, believe all things, hope all things, endure all things?

Look at the "Love Chapter" — chapter 13 of First Corinthians. *The Amplified Bible* describes this kind of love in a dynamic way. In verses 4-8 it says:

> **Love endures long and is patient and kind; love never is envious nor boils over with jealousy; is not boastful or vainglorious, does not display itself haughtily.**
>
> **It is not conceited — arrogant and inflated with pride; it is not rude (unmannerly), and does not act unbecomingly. Love [God's love in us] does not insist on its own rights or its own way, for it is not self-seeking; it is not touchy or fretful or resentful; it takes no account of the evil done to it — pays no attention to a suffered wrong.**

It does not rejoice at injustice and unrighteousness, but rejoices when right and truth prevail.

Love bears up under anything and everything that comes, is ever ready to believe the best of every person, its hopes are fadeless under all circumstances and it endures everything [without weakening].

Love never fails — never fades out or becomes obsolete or comes to an end.

Of course, no one but God does all of these things all of the time, but as Christian parents we should strive to be like Him.

Be Honest With Your Children

It's really important for us as parents to be honest with our kids.

When we fail them in any way or do wrong to them, we should be person enough to admit it and say, "Honey, I messed up. I'm sorry. Will you forgive me?"

If we lose our temper and speak harshly to them, we should apologize. Sooner or later, they will find out that we aren't perfect anyway.

You may say, "But if I represent God and He doesn't make mistakes, won't my kids think less of God if they see me make a mistake?"

Look at it this way: if a person does you wrong, do you think less of him if he comes to you and apologizes for it? Of course not. We usually think less of the person who doesn't apologize.

When you admit having made a mistake to your kids and ask them to forgive you, you are setting an example for them to follow. They see that when a person flubs up, the right thing to do is to ask forgiveness. They also realize that messing up doesn't make them unlovable.

31

Your making mistakes and apologizing for them doesn't reflect badly on God, but making mistakes and pretending you are perfect does. Children can sense hypocrisy a mile away. If you start strutting around, pretending you are perfect, your kids will know you are a phony. And sooner or later they will reject that hypocrisy.

Now notice we didn't say you should act like you *are* God. We said you should act *like* God. There is a big difference here. Some parents are tyrants who bully their kids into obeying them. But that's not how God deals with us. He doesn't beat us over the head, call us names, or tell us how stupid and no-good we are. And we aren't to act that way either!

The apostle Paul said:

> **Therefore be imitators of God — copy Him and follow His example — as well-beloved children [imitate their father].**
>
> **Ephesians 5:1 AMP**

Practice What You Preach

We are to be imitators of God, but the only way we can do that is by knowing God personally.

For years parents have been proving that the old practice of *Do as I say, not as I do* just doesn't work. You can talk until you are blue in the face, but if you don't practice what you preach, you might as well save your breath. Your kids will turn a deaf ear to what you are saying, and they will imitate what you are doing.

If you want your kids to love God and serve Him, you first have to love and serve Him yourself. You can't show them what it means to walk and talk with God if you haven't been down that road yourself. You have to get to know God before you can truly show them what He is like.

The better you know God, the more you will be like Him and the more your children will see Him in you. There is no way you can raise a successful Christian child if you yourself are not a successful Christian.

Whether you like it or not, you are your children's picture of God. The better you know Him, the more you can be like Him. And the more you are like Him, the more your children can know Who God is and how much He loves them.

4

Help Your Children Know God

Maybe you are thinking something like this: "I'm a Christian and I love the Lord, but I don't really know how to help my kids know Who He is. I pray for them and I try to live a godly life before them. What else can I do?"

Well, how do we get to know God, really know Him?

Think of it like putting an airplane together. Every part is vital in order to get it off the ground and into the air.

But one person might say, "Well, you know, the wings are the most important part. It takes wings for an airplane to fly."

Someone else may say, "No, the engine is the most important part. An airplane won't fly without an engine."

Still others say, "No, it's the rudder," or, "No, it's the instruments," or, "No, it's the landing gear."

The truth is, every part is vital and important. All the parts have to work together before the airplane will be able to fly.

Well, that's how it is when you are trying to help your kids know God. There are several ways to do it, but no one way can do it alone. *All* the ways are needed in order for them to truly know God.

Get To Know God
Through Prayer and His Word

One of the most important ways we can get to know God is by spending time each day praying and talking with

Him. Some people mistakenly think they have to spend so many minutes in prayer each day to earn points with God. But that's not how it works.

As you talk with God, you get to know Him. You become sensitive to His voice and to His presence. Notice, we didn't say you talk *to* God; we said you talk *with* God. Prayer is not a narration; it's talking back and forth with Him. You talk *and* you listen while God talks to your heart and spirit. Meaningful prayer is not a one-sided conversation, but a two-way exchange.

It is also important that you read the Bible every day. The Bible is God's guidebook. It tells you about Him, and it outlines how you are to live and act as His child. It is also God's promise book. No matter what you face, He has a promise of provision for your need. That's why reading God's Word every day is so important. By reading and studying His Word, you can know His promises and claim them in faith before trouble comes.

When you pray and read the Word every day, you are also renewing your mind.

> **Be not conformed to this world: but be ye transformed by the renewing of your mind, that ye may prove what is that good, and acceptable, and perfect, will of God.**
>
> **Romans 12:2**

W.E. Vine in his *Expository Dictionary of New Testament Words*[1] defines the renewing of your mind as "the adjustment of the moral and spiritual vision and thinking to the mind of God, which is designed to have a transforming effect upon the life." According to his definition, it will do you little good to know what God expects of you unless you

---

[1](Old Tappan, New Jersey: Fleming H. Revell, 1966), p. 279.

start doing it. That means obedience. Listen to God in prayer, back it up with His Word, then do what He tells you to do.

The secret of obedience lies in learning to know Jesus Christ better and better. That's why you have to pray and read God's Word every day. It puts you in touch with Him and strengthens your spirit so that you grow stronger and stronger. You may still struggle at times, but as you learn to walk in the spirit, obeying God will become easier.

The Importance of Family Devotions

This same principle works in your family's spiritual life. When you pray and read the Word together, when you talk about God and what it means to be a Christian, your family will get stronger spiritually.

Most kids don't have the self-discipline to sit down by themselves every day and read the Bible and pray. They just won't do it. But you can make sure they know God and His Word by praying with them, reading the Bible to them, talking about God with them and having regular family devotions.

In the book of Deuteronomy, God commanded the Israelites to teach their children His laws, and He told them how to do it. He said:

> **And these words, which I command thee this day, shall be in thine heart:**
>
> **And thou shalt teach them diligently unto thy children, and shalt talk of them when thou sittest in thine house, and when thou walkest by the way, and when thou liest down, and when thou risest up.**
>
> **And thou shalt bind them for a sign upon thine hand, and they shall be as frontlets between thine eyes.**
>
> **And thou shalt write them upon the posts of thy house, and on thy gates.**
>
> **Deuteronomy 6:6-9**

God is simply saying this: "I want you to fill your family life with talk about Me and My Word. I want you to talk to your children about Me and My commandments every day. While you are working around the house, when you go for a walk, when you get ready for bed, or when you get up in the morning, teach your children about Me."

Our daughter, Candas, used to be afraid to go to school when she was in the second or third grade. On the way to school, Buddy would drill Second Timothy 1:7 into her: "God has not given me the spirit of fear; but of power, and of love, and of a sound mind." They drilled on that verse, along with another verse in Jude 20: **...ye, beloved, building up yourselves on your most holy faith, praying in the Holy Ghost.** Those two Scriptures, the first two Candas learned, helped her through school and had a major impact on her life.

Unfortunately, some people never talk about God in their homes. The only time they mention Him is when something terrible happens. Then they wonder why their kids feel uncomfortable talking about Him.

God says you are to talk about Him and His Word naturally, in your everyday conversation. Wherever you are and whatever you are doing, if an opportunity comes along for you to talk about God, do it. As you get to know Him, it will become second nature for you to talk about Him. In fact, it will be difficult to talk without mentioning His name.

You may say, "How can I do that without sounding phony to my kids?"

Suppose an unexpected bill comes in and you don't have the money to pay it. Talk to your children about it. Show them in the Bible where God gave the Israelites manna in the wilderness. (Ex. 16.) Point out that if He provided for them, you can trust Him to provide for you because He is the same yesterday, today and forever. (Heb. 13:8.) Then have them pray with you and ask God to provide money to help you pay the bill.

Or suppose someone in your family is sick. Ask your children to pray with you for that one who is ill. You can pray together that God's healing power will be manifested.

Teach your family these powerful truths.

Prayer Binds You Together

Having family devotions will fulfill your children's need for daily spiritual food.

Now, you may be thinking, *Oh no, not family devotions!* Maybe you have tried them before, but it just didn't work. Maybe the little ones got bored in three minutes and the teenagers were resentful for a week. So you wanted to forget the whole thing!

Family devotions can be a wonderful time if you handle them right, but some people think family devotions are getting together at home to play church. That gives Mom and Dad a great chance to preach at the kids. But that isn't how it should be. Your goal is not to train up "religious" kids, but kids who have a personal relationship with Jesus Christ.

Family devotions teach your children that God is important — so important that you set aside a time each day just to be with Him, to talk with Him and to learn of Him from His Word. Your children can sense the relationship you have with God.

Even though Buddy's work schedule didn't follow the normal eight to five pattern, we made it a family priority to have devotions every morning. Sometimes everyone would just barely drag themselves down the stairs because they were so sleepy. Once everyone was there, Buddy would read from the Word, share a little bit, then have everybody pray in English about whatever they had on their heart. Then Buddy would wind it up by having everybody pray in the Holy Spirit.

Even though the devotion might have seemed dry at the time, later on it showed fruit. Once our daughters got into junior high, some of their girlfriends found out about our devotions and started coming to them. Some of the girls got saved and filled with the Holy Spirit!

During those years, we raised four other girls, who lived with us off and on, besides our own. Whoever was living in our house at the time always had to come to devotions. I remember in particular one of the girls' friends who had been kicked out of her house by her mother. She immediately came to us, probably because she knew we would take her in. In the morning, she would listen to her rock and roll music while getting dressed, then she would come down to devotions. She knew we cared about her, and the devotions just seemed to reinforce how much God loved her, too.

Your family devotions should grow naturally out of your own love for God and His Word as you share that love and joy with your family. Remember, devotions don't have to be long and boring. You can make them short, interesting and fun!

Also, remember what the passage in Deuteronomy 6 says. First, God said, **These words, which I command thee this day, shall be in thine heart** (v. 6). Then He said, **Thou shalt teach them diligently unto thy children** (v. 7). That's why you first have to personally know God and His Word, so you can share that knowledge with your children.

You don't have to be a Bible scholar or have all the answers before you can have devotions with your family. But you can't share the joy of salvation and of serving God with them if you haven't experienced it yourself. You can't teach them to trust God if you aren't learning to trust Him yourself.

Having devotions gives you the opportunity to let your kids share in your own spiritual struggles, and you can share in theirs. You can talk together about different things in your life: the problems you are having, the things God has shown you in the past and the joy you know by serving Him. And you can pray for each other.

When you pray, don't try to sound like a seminary professor. Just pray simple, honest prayers in your own words about your own needs. It does our kids good to hear us confess our needs, our failures and our hurts to God, and then to hear us praise Him for His answers and provisions.

You can also show your children how special they are to you by taking their needs and concerns to God in prayer. Sometimes parents can think their children's worries as too trivial to pray about. Those things may seem unimportant to you, but they are extremely important to your kids.

One of the greatest things you can do for them is pray for them. When they hear you speak their names and talk to God about their personal problems, they will never forget it.

In one family the father kept a little black notebook where he wrote down his children's prayer requests — anything they wanted their daddy to pray about. After growing up, one of those kids said this about it:

"That notebook was very special to my brothers and sisters and me. It symbolized the time and prayer that our dad devoted to us. We knew our prayer requests were important to him, and he would pray about them until the problems were taken care of. For Dad to take our needs to Almighty God like that, we knew he loved us an awful lot."

You know the old saying: "The family that prays together stays together." There is something about confessing our needs to one another and praying for one another that binds us together and helps us love each other more.

You can do lots of things to make your family devotions meaningful and fun. But remember, there is no ironclad rule that says you must have them a certain way at a certain time. Work out the time and way that is best for your family, according to their needs.

The important thing is that you make devotions an essential part of your family's daily life. Your children need to be taught about God and His Word, and He has given you the responsibility to do it.

Take Your Family to Church

Another important way you can teach your family about God is by going to church regularly. We can't emphasize church attendance enough. You need a body of Bible-believing people holding you and your family up in prayer in order to make it in today's world.

Now, some may say, "Oh, I don't need to go to church. I read my Bible and pray, and God teaches me everything I need to know." But when a family is content not to have a definite time and place to worship, that's a family which rarely worships at all.

God doesn't save us to be spiritual "Lone Rangers." When you accept Jesus as Savior, you are born into the family of God, the Body of Christ and the kingdom of heaven. Jesus came to establish His Church, and He told us exactly how it was to operate. Nowhere did He say anything about Christians going off and operating on their own.

In Hebrews 10:25 AMP we read how we are to join together with other believers:

> Not forsaking or neglecting to assemble together [as believers], as is the habit of some people, but admonishing — warning, urging and encouraging — one another, and all the more faithfully as you see the day approaching.

We are to be part of a church so we can encourage one another, pray for one another, teach one another and help one another. Jesus said:

> Again I say unto you, That if two of you shall agree on earth as touching any thing that they shall ask, it shall be done for them of my Father which is in heaven.
>
> For where two or three are gathered together in my name, there am I in the midst of them.
>
> Matthew 18:19,20

The problem with Christians who go off and do their own thing is that when they run into problems, there is no one to help them. There is no one to hold them accountable or to pray for them. Jesus said there is power in numbers. Where one alone has trouble fighting Satan, two or three believers together can put him on the run.

Some people have the idea that they go to church to pay their dues. They say: "If I go to church, that means I'm a good person. If I don't go, I'm not being good."

But that's not why we go to church. We go because we are part of the Body of Christ, and that makes us accountable to each other. We are to fellowship and worship together. Then we can receive a direct word from God, and we can benefit from the spiritual wisdom and experiences of other members of the Body.

Now you may say, "But Sunday is the only time I get to see my husband. He's not a Christian, and he works six days a week. How can I take my kids and go off to church, leaving him behind?"

Or maybe you say, "I have to work on Sunday. What should I do?"

We aren't so concerned that you be in church every Sunday as we are that you and your children are in church — period. If you feel you can't spend two hours away from your husband (or wife) on Sunday morning, maybe you could at least go for an hour during Sunday school. Or maybe you could go to the mid-week service or a Bible study during the week. First, get your children involved in your church's youth activities. Then, if you can, join an adult Bible class.

The day of the week is not that important. You just need to receive the teaching of God's Word and find a place of fellowship for you and your family. You need to be committed to a local church body, to be a part of it and to be there as much as you can. If you get so excited about church and God's people that you just bubble over, maybe your husband will want to go with you to see what's happening.

Just remember: attending church is important. And if you are in a position where it is difficult for you to attend, pray and ask God to help you. Ask Him to give you wisdom about the situation. Ask Him to help you arrange your priorities in the proper way. Ask Him to give you some creative ways to be an active part of His Body.

Find a Bible-Believing Church

It's important that you go to church, but it's also important which church you go to. Don't just go to any church. Find one that preaches the entire Word of God. Romans 10:17 says, **Faith cometh by hearing, and hearing by the word of God.** When the Word is preached under the anointing of the Holy Spirit, faith will spring forth from your heart and enable you to believe God for answers to your problems and needs.

So listen to God. There may be many good churches in your area, but you should go where He wants you to go.

Then, once you have found the right church for you and your family, attend regularly. Support it with your attendance, your tithes and offerings, and your talents.

As much as possible, take your kids to church yourself; don't just send them. There are some parents who see Sunday school as a kind of free baby-sitting service. They send their kids away on Sunday mornings so they can sleep in. But if you want your kids to go to church, you take them!

Your children need church. They need the friendship and influence of other Christian kids with activities they can participate in. They need to hear the preaching of the Word and see God working miracles in people's lives. In church they can see sinners saved. They can see lives changed. They can see the hungry filled with the Holy Ghost. They can be part of a missions program that reaches out to the lost overseas and here at home. Your church can fulfill all these needs and be a vital part of your children's spiritual growth.

But let's add a word of caution here: don't think your church can replace you, because it can't. Too many parents turn over the responsibility for teaching their kids the Word of God to a church. God gave that job to you as the parent. The church is there to add to what you do — not replace you.

And going to church should not replace the family activities you share. So many young people have said they got turned off by church because their families never did anything together except go to church. None of us ever has enough time to do all the things we need to do. But don't leave out family activities, especially not because of church. That will turn off your kids quicker than anything.

45

Church activities are important, but don't let them replace your family fun times. Memories are a lifetime investment. You need to set aside the time and money for special family activities. When your kids are grown, these are the times they will remember.

Lead Your Children to Jesus Christ

The greatest joy you can have as a parent is to lead your children to accept Jesus Christ as their personal Lord and Savior.

We experienced joy when a baby was born to us, but there was no greater joy than seeing our kids born into the kingdom of God. Our earthly life is mortal or temporal, but our life in Jesus Christ is immortal or eternal. In this life on earth we can only be together for a few years, but in heaven we will be together for eternity. That's why leading a child to accept Jesus Christ is so joyous.

Many parents feel inadequate to lead their kids to the Lord, so they let the church handle that job. But leading a child to Jesus Christ isn't difficult. The Gospel is so simple that even a small child can understand it.

When praying for your children, you should always ask God to save them at the earliest possible age, even the little ones.

Someone may ask, "But do you really think little children need to be saved? How old should a child be?"

When a child is old enough to lie or steal or curse or deliberately disobey, he is old enough to get saved. When she is old enough to understand the difference between right and wrong, she is old enough to realize she has done wrong and needs to be forgiven.

It is important that we try to reach our children as early as possible. All three of our children were saved by the time they were six years old. A child is easier to reach for Jesus Christ because his mind is still in the formative stage. He hasn't yet experienced the sin and sorrow of the world, and his heart is still open to the things of God.

So you ask, "How do I lead my child to Jesus?"

First, you have to know that child. You have to talk with him and understand what he is thinking and feeling. As you spend time together, you will start to feel when he is ready, and you can encourage him to ask questions.

A child comes to Jesus the same way you came. When you sense your child is really interested in accepting Him, explain salvation in terms he can understand. You don't have to go into all the theological nitty-gritty. The important thing is that he knows God loves him.

Tell him this: God loves us so much that He sent His only Son, Jesus, to earth to die so that we could be saved. We are all born as sinners, and we need God's forgiveness. Because Jesus died for our sins, God will forgive us if we ask Him. He will wash our hearts clean and put His Spirit within us to live with us forever.

Let your child ask questions, then try to answer them honestly. When you feel he understands the plan of salvation, ask if he would like to have God forgive him of his sins. If he says yes, pray a simple prayer with him (like the prayer we gave you in the first chapter of this book).

Don't pressure your child into saying yes. If he doesn't want to ask God for forgiveness, realize that he is simply not ready. Wait for another opportunity. But continue teaching him and praying for him.

It is very important that at some point you ask your children whether or not they have accepted Jesus as their Lord and Savior. Many parents assume that because their kids are being raised in church they have accepted Him, but that's not always the case. Sometimes after people are saved, they say, "I was raised in church, but I never really accepted Jesus until today."

So don't assume your kids are saved — ask them! It's not enough to know about God. Each one of us must know Him personally in order to be saved.

Teach your children to pray. Instill in them a love and respect for God's Word. Take them to Sunday school and church. But don't stop there. Lead them to make the most important decision of their lives by accepting Jesus Christ as their Lord and Savior. There is no greater gift you can give your kids than the gift of salvation.

What will it profit you to gain the whole world if you lose the eternal souls of your own children through neglect or indifference? And what good will it do to provide them with everything they want or need if you neglect the most important thing in life — their salvation?

No matter what ages your kids may be, start now to talk about God and pray with them, to study His Word and attend church together. It will bring results — and you will never regret it.

Your Harvest Is Coming in Due Season

Teaching your children about God is not always an easy job. We all have days when we wonder if we are doing a good job, if anything we are saying is getting through to them, or if it will make a difference in their lives. But we promise you, it will.

Every prayer you pray, every family devotional time you have, every truth about God that you put in your children's hearts is like a little seed you are planting in their lives. Sure, it's hard work. It's a daily task. You have to keep planting and watering those seeds. You have to keep nurturing those tender shoots. Sometimes you have to prune a little here and cut a little there. And it's painful. It's tough. It's a lifetime commitment. But if you do these things, someday those seeds will bear fruit.

The harvest may not come when you think it should. Strong winds may blow, and heavy rains may fall. At times you may think those seeds have died in the ground. But someday you will see a harvest of righteousness in that child's life.

> **For as the rain and snow come down from the heavens, and return not there again, but water the earth and make it bring forth and sprout, that it may give seed to the sower and bread to the eater,**
>
> **So shall My word be that goes forth out of My mouth; it shall not return to Me void — without producing any effect, useless — but it shall accomplish that which I please and purpose, and it shall prosper in the thing for which I sent it.**
>
> **Isaiah 55:10,11 AMP**

Remember, Proverbs 22:6 says, **Train up a child in the way he should go [and in keeping with his individual gift or bent], and when he is old he will not depart from it** (AMP). And Ecclesiastes 11:1 says, **Cast your bread upon the waters, for you will find it after many days** (AMP).

All these verses are saying the same thing: *God is faithful!* When you obey Him and do all you can to raise your kids to love and serve Him, He will honor your efforts. When you plant His Word in their hearts and lives, it will not return void. It will bear fruit — not necessarily in *your* time, but in God's time.

> **They that sow in tears shall reap in joy.**
>
> **He that goeth forth and weepeth, bearing precious seed, shall doubtless come again with rejoicing, bringing his sheaves with him.**
>
> **Psalm 126:5,6**

There is a harvest coming if you don't give up as a parent. So keep teaching your children God's Word. Keep praying for them and with them. Keep taking them to church. Be faithful. It will pay off in eternal dividends.

5

Teach Your Children Who They Are

In Matthew's gospel, chapter 18, the disciples asked Jesus which of them would be most important in His kingdom. Can't you see these men standing around like a bunch of little kids, arguing about who was the greatest?

We can just imagine one of them saying something like this: "Well, you know, I must be the most important because I help Jesus with the preaching. Remember when He sent us out two by two? I held meetings in several towns, and there were all kinds of miracles! I must be the greatest!"

But Peter probably said, "You know, boys, I'm Jesus' right-hand man. He wouldn't be where He is today if it weren't for me. I think I'm the most important."

Then Judas spoke up and said, "No, I'm the most important because I'm the treasurer. Money talks, you know. I finance this whole operation, so if it weren't for me, we wouldn't be in business."

The discussion could have gone on and on, with each disciple telling why he thinks he is the most important. Finally, someone says, "Let's go ask Jesus." So they did.

Jesus answered them by calling a little child to Him and saying:

> **Verily I say unto you, Except ye be converted, and become as little children, ye shall not enter into the kingdom of heaven.**

Whosoever therefore shall humble himself as this little child, the same is greatest in the kingdom of heaven.

And whoso shall receive one such little child in my name receiveth me.

But whoso shall offend one of these little ones which believe in me, it were better for him that a millstone were hanged about his neck, and that he were drowned in the depth of the sea.

Woe unto the world because of offences! for it must needs be that offences come; but woe to that man by whom the offence cometh!

Matthew 18:3-7

God loves children. Jesus said if we are to enter the kingdom of God we must become like little children, and the one who is like a child is the greatest in the kingdom of heaven. Throughout the Bible, God calls us His children and says He is our Father. He tells us how precious we are and how much He loves us. And that's the kind of parents we are to be.

Children Are Valuable and Precious

In the past few chapters we have looked at some of the most important things you can do for your children:

- Know God yourself.

- Pray for them.

- Let them know Who God is.

- Help them to know God personally.

Now we want to add to that list. Another of the most important things you can do for your children is:

- Teach them who they are in Christ Jesus.

Psalm 127:3 says, **Lo, children are an heritage of the Lord: and the fruit of the womb is his reward.** A heritage is an inheritance, a legacy, something received from a parent. The psalmist was saying that children belong to God. First, they are His, then He gives them back to us.

Your children need to feel that they are loved unconditionally, that they are of great worth — both to you and to God. You are to love and respect them as God's gifts to you. According to Deuteronomy 28:4, children are one of the blessings God bestows on us.

Every child born into this world is a one-of-a-kind divine creation, a unique person who is precious to God. He loves each of us so much that He gave the greatest, most precious gift He had — His only Son — so we could be with Him throughout eternity. God doesn't start loving us just when we accept Him as Savior. He loved us even before we were born.

Let's look at how the psalmist describes our God and how He sees us:

> For You did form my inward parts, You did knit me together in my mother's womb.
>
> I will confess and praise You, for You are fearfully wonderful, and for the awful wonder of my birth! Wonderful are Your works, and that my inner self knows right well.
>
> My frame was not hidden from You, when I was being formed in secret and intricately and curiously wrought (as if embroidered with various colors) in the depths of the earth [a region of darkness and mystery].
>
> Your eyes saw my unformed substance, and in Your book all the days of my life were written, before ever they took shape, when as yet there was none of them.
>
> How precious and weighty also are Your thoughts to me, O God! How vast is the sum of them!
>
> If I could count them, they are more in number than the sand.
>
> **Psalm 139:13-18 AMP**

This shows how precious our children are to God. Even before they were born, God had a plan all written out for their lives. He sent Jesus to die so they could have eternal life.

Do you feel that way about your children? Do you let them know how much you love and value them? Have you told them how much God loves and values them? If not, you should.

In chapter 3 we talked about how we are God's representatives to our children and how important it is that we show them Who God is. But it's equally as important that we show them who they are in Jesus Christ.

No Child Is an "Accident"

We have heard parents talk about the birth of unplanned children as if they were accidents. But there are no accidents with God. He doesn't make mistakes. Even before a baby is born, God has a plan and a purpose written down in His book for that child. God's thoughts of love go out to him constantly.

Every human life is of precious value to God — special, wonderful, full of potential. God alone creates life, and every life is precious to Him.

Maybe you didn't plan your child, but God did. He wanted to bless you with that baby. He wanted to enrich your life. And that's what you need to teach your children: that they are special blessings from God, that they are precious and deeply loved — by you and by Him.

You need to teach your kids that they were made in the image of God (Gen. 1:26,27); that God loves them and died for them (John 3:16); that no matter how "good" or "bad" they may act, God will always love them (Rom. 5:8); that He will never leave them nor forsake them (Heb. 13:5). And if the Creator of the whole universe loves them that much, they really are somebody important!

This is why we should never say to our kids things like, "You're stupid," or "You'll never amount to anything," or "You're just like your Aunt So-and-so." God doesn't think these things about us, and we don't have the right to say them to our kids. After all, they are His property. They belong to Him. Every good and perfect gift is from God. (James 1:17.)

Love Isn't Enough

You may ask, "Why is it so important that my child know who he is in Jesus? I love my child. Isn't that enough?"

It would be great if we could tell you that just loving your child is enough to help him become the person God wants him to be. But the truth is, we live in a sinful world, and we as Christian parents are not perfect yet.

It is so easy to get caught up in the false values of the world. People without the Lord Jesus spend their time and effort running after beauty, wealth, power and intellect. And if we aren't careful, we could teach our children these false values rather than God's values.

According to the world, Jesus was a loser. He wasn't a landowner or a wealthy businessman. He was never given any honors or awards. He had a simple education. He hung around with blue-collar workers, hookers, outcasts and losers. For the last three years of His life He didn't hold a steady job. He never left His own country to travel around the world, and He knew very few celebrities or national leaders. He was arrested and executed for being a fraud and a troublemaker. His friends and family deserted Him, and He was even buried in a borrowed grave.

Do you see how false the values of the world are? The world says Jesus was a loser, but God's Word says He was the greatest Winner Who ever lived. And because He won, we can win, too!

During the last few hours before He was crucified, Jesus prayed to His heavenly Father for everyone who would believe on Him. He prayed, **I do not ask that You will take them out of the world, but that You will keep and protect them from the evil [one]** (John 17:15 AMP).

That's the kind of prayer we should pray for our children — not that they be isolated from the world, but that they be protected from evil in the world.

We are all influenced by our culture. We are *in* the world, but we don't have to be *of* the world. The world says that because your skin is a different color, or because you don't do as well in school as other kids, or because your clothes aren't as fancy as someone else's, you aren't as good as everybody else.

The world says there is something wrong with you. But God says: "I made you. I love you. I know everything there is about you. You are a person of worth to Me. I even died for you."

Your children will come under attack from the world, because the world is out to destroy them any way it can. That's why it is so important that they hear the truth about themselves from you, their parent. They have to be taught that it doesn't matter what the world says about them. The thing that matters is what God says about them.

God loves everyone equally. He doesn't look at how much money you have in your pocket. He doesn't care what kind of car you drive or how big your house is. God cares about the kind of person you are on the inside, not the way you look on the outside.

So many of us adults were wounded in our spirits as children, and we are still walking around with these hurts inside us. Maybe someone said cruel things about us or treated us in a mean way. Maybe the kids made fun of us because we were poor. Maybe a teacher told us we weren't very smart. Or maybe our parents said things that were painful or even brutal.

We grew up believing those lies. Because of the things that were said, we think we aren't really as smart or pretty or good as other people. We feel bad about who we are, and if not careful we will pass those bad feelings on to our kids. We will treat them the way we were treated.

The truth is, we are sons and daughters of the King of the universe. We have wealth beyond measure. We have a home made of pure gold and robes of pure white to wear. God thinks so highly of us that He considers us His righteousness. Second Corinthians 5:21 in *The New International Version* says, **God made him** [Jesus] **who had no sin to be sin for us, so that in him we might become the righteousness of God.**

These are the kinds of things you need to be telling your children. Whether we believe them or not — God's Word says they are true. And as His representative, you need to tell your kids over and over again who they are in Christ Jesus.

True Self-Esteem Comes From God

The world calls this "building self-esteem." But the focus of the world is on "me," not on Jesus Christ. In the world's thinking, all that counts is "what I can do" and "who I am." But that's not true self-esteem.

The Bible says we are all sinners. (Rom. 3:23.) We needed the cleansing blood of Jesus Christ. (1 John 1:7.) Our righteousness was no more than filthy rags. (Isa. 64:6.) Without God's forgiveness, we were condemned and on our way to hell. But when we accepted Jesus Christ, He gave us His worth.

> **But as many as received him, to them gave he power to become the sons [and daughters] of God, even to them that believe on his name.**
>
> **John 1:12**

This is where true self-esteem and worth come from: our being sons and daughters of God, heirs of God and joint-heirs with Jesus Christ. (Rom. 8:15-17.) Like the apostle Paul, we can say:

> **I am crucified with Christ: nevertheless I live; yet not I, but Christ liveth in me: and the life which I now live in the flesh I live by the faith of the Son of God, who loved me, and gave himself for me.**
>
> **Galatians 2:20**

As a parent, if you are walking around today with a load of hurt inside you, kicking yourself and putting yourself down, feeling like you aren't as good as the rest of the world, you need to take a hard look at what the Word of God says about you.

Every time those negative thoughts come to your mind, rebuke them. Quit believing them. Start telling yourself what the Bible says about you. Start believing that you are who the Bible says you are, not who the world says you are.

How sad it is for the child who "gets it" from everyone, even his own family. His home isn't a place of refuge from the cruel world. His parents aren't his friends and defenders who believe in him and encourage him.

There have been many Christian homes where the parents didn't put their children down, but they didn't build them up either. They just failed to teach them who they are and can be in Jesus Christ.

We have to see our children the way God sees them.

We have to teach our children what the Word of God says about them.

We have to help our children find the special gifts God has given them and the plan He has for their lives.

We have to help our children develop according to how God wants them to grow.

If we as parents fail to do these things, the consequences can be tragic. So many kids are messed up today because no one really taught them about God. No one ever prayed with them, talked with them and really listened to them. No one ever taught them who they are in Jesus Christ.

Yes, they are loved, but the message the world gives them may seem louder and stronger than the message they get at home. The world tells them they are unacceptable and unlovable, ugly and bad. And somewhere along the line, if they believe those lies, they may give up. They may quit trying.

This is why so many of our young people are using drugs and alcohol, why so many girls are starving themselves to be beautiful, why so many are getting pregnant. They can't seem to say no to the world's crowd that wants them to take drugs or who promises love in exchange for sex. They don't know how to cope.

But we parents can make a difference. We can help our children grow up to be men and women of God.

6

Seven Ways To Help Your Children Grow

In the previous chapters we have shared with you some things you could do in raising your kids to walk with Jesus Christ. Throughout this book we will discuss other things you can do.

There are some specific ways you can help your children to grow. So let's look at them.

Tell Your Children Every Day How Much You Love and Appreciate Them

From the moment you know you are going to have a baby, start thinking of that child as a person of great worth. Praise and thank God for blessing you with that child.

As soon as your children are born, tell them how precious they are. Let them know how much they mean to you. What a special gift of God they are!

Tell them how much God loves them and what wonderful things He has promised to do for them.

Tell them how proud and thankful you are that they are yours.

Speak the Good More Than the Bad

Your children will sin. They will fail and disappoint you, because they are human — just like you are. But don't dwell on the bad. Forgive as God forgives. Discipline them the way that God disciplines you — with respect and love.

Let's look at Psalm 103:8-14 from *The New International Version*. It tells us how to treat our children.

> **The Lord is compassionate and
>   gracious,
>   slow to anger, abounding in love.
> He will not always accuse,
>   nor will he harbor his anger forever;
> he does not treat us as our sins deserve
>   or repay us according to our
>   iniquities.
> For as high as the heavens are above
>   the earth,
>   so great is his love for those who fear
>   him;
> as far as the east is from the west,
>   so far has he removed our
>   transgressions from us.
> As a father has compassion on his
>   children,
>   so the Lord has compassion on those
>   who fear him;
> for he knows how we are formed,
>   he remembers that we are dust.**

Tell Your Children That They Are Winners in Jesus Christ

The world compares one person with another. It decides who the winners are and who the losers are. Even in our schools, children must compete with each other for grades, honors and activities.

But we don't have to compete for God's love and attention. He loves us just the way we are. We all fall short in one area or another. We all have weaknesses and strengths. But God accepts us for who we are and pronounces us "Winners!"

And that's what your children need to hear. When the world rejects them and puts them down, keep telling them that they are winners in Jesus Christ.

Help Your Children Discover Their God-Given Gifts

Each of us has abilities and talents God has given us to use for His glory and work. As your children grow, help them discover what their abilities are and develop them for use in God's kingdom.

Is your son musical? Help him develop that talent through music lessons.

Does your daughter have the gift of helping others? Provide her with opportunities to use her gift.

Is he a good speaker? Encourage him to take classes in school that will develop and strengthen that gift.

But most important, teach your children that all their gifts and abilities are from God — because He loves them and wants to help them serve Him.

Help Your Children Overcome Their Handicaps

All of us have handicaps in some way. Sometimes the world causes us to have them. Sometimes they come from our wrong thinking. Sometimes we are born with them. Some handicaps are physical, some are mental, some are emotional.

But it's vitally important that you help your children overcome their handicaps.

Maybe one child has developed bad eating habits that are affecting his health. Teach him that his body is the temple of the Holy Ghost. (1 Cor. 6:19.) Provide good food for him. Encourage him to exercise. And pray for him every day!

Maybe another child has an emotional problem, or difficulties in school, or even something as simple as crooked teeth. The problem may seem small to you, but it may be affecting your child in a major way.

Whatever the problems, seek God's wisdom and guidance in helping your kids to deal with the things that are preventing them from being all God desires them to be.

Our handicaps have nothing to do with our worth to God or His love for us. But they can hold us back. They can cheat us of our joy, keep us from doing our best and make us feel bad about ourselves. When they do, we need God's help to overcome them.

Teach Your Children the Principles of Hard Work and Responsibility

During the Depression many people had to work both inside and outside the home. In those days children were expected to help out where they could. But today many parents feel they are being too hard on their kids if they ask them to help out around the house.

God's Word says:

> ...make it your ambition and definitely endeavor to live quietly and peacefully, to mind your own affairs, and to work with your hands, as we charged you;
>
> So that you may bear yourselves becomingly, be correct and honorable and command the respect of the

outside world, being (self-supporting,) dependent on nobody and having need of nothing.
1 Thessalonians 4:11,12 AMP

In the beginning, God gave man work to do:

The Lord God took the man and put him in the Garden of Eden to work it and take care of it.
Genesis 2:15 NIV

Work is built into the very nature of man. God created us to work. It's part of who we are and what we are. It gives us a sense of purpose and makes us feel good about ourselves. So it's important that we teach our children to work.

When your kids are small, start giving them jobs to do. Make them responsible for helping around the house. As they get older, expect more from them. Teach them that work is good, that it's important and ordained by God.

Prepare Your Children for the Future

Only God knows exactly what the future holds, but you should prepare your children for the things they will most likely face.

Start teaching them when they are young about how to overcome the temptations of drugs, sex and rebellion that they will face as teenagers.

As you help them discover God's plan and purposes for their lives, you can help them prepare to someday leave home, get a job, or continue their education or training.

Each day you can help them grow and become the kind of husband, wife or parent that God intends for them to be.

Tell your children before they go through difficult times what they are going to be up against. Share with them your memories about these times in your life and how God helped you overcome them. Pray with them. Talk with them. But, most importantly, listen to them. Keep the lines of communication and love open.

Every teenager who ever lived thinks his parents never faced the kinds of pressures and difficulties he faces. But that isn't true. We all are human. We all have been through these changing times of life. And we all can help our kids prepare for the future.

Your children are worth your very best efforts. And as a parent you can make a difference in their lives.

You can instill a love for God in their hearts and a desire to serve Him.

You can teach them Who God is and who they are in relation to Him.

You can help them prepare for the future and help them through those difficult times.

You can pray for them, praise them, push them and prepare them. And you have God's promise of help as you do.

7
How To Discipline in Love

My parents had certain rules and standards that I was expected to follow. When I would chose to disobey the rules or violate the standards, I knew that there were consequences. When the consequence came, whether it was a spanking or a privilege withheld, it didn't come as a surprise.

Since my Daddy, Kenneth Hagin, is a minister, he was away from home a lot, preaching and evangelizing, and my Mom was really the disciplinarian in our home. But I do remember two or three times that I did get a spanking from Daddy. I especially remember one time in particular.

I was five or six years old at the time, and we were living in Van, Texas. We had an outdoor toilet, and my Daddy was busy helping some men put a sewer system in so they could run some indoor plumbing up to the house. Outside they had great big concrete pipes that hadn't been put into the ground yet. My Daddy had told my brother, Ken, and me not to play on them because they could crack if we happened to roll them together. He also told us that if we didn't stay off of them he would spank us.

Eventually our curiousity got the best of us, and Ken and I climbed up on those big concrete pipes. We were having a good old time when one of them cracked. Because my Daddy was a man who was true to his word, we got a spanking. He never spanked us in anger; instead, he disciplined us with his word.

Oh, he gave us a couple of licks with a belt all right, but he would always sit Ken and me down to ask us if we knew why we were being disciplined. Then we had to tell him what we did that was disobedient and share with him what the Word says in Ephesians chapter 6, verses 1 and 2, about honoring and obeying your parents in the Lord.

Then, to make sure we understood why we were being disciplined, he would repeat to us what the disobedience was that we had done, why we were being disciplined for it and what the Word said about it.

I cried easily, so sometimes I would start crying. But one thing he and Mom never did was let me cry for a long time. After they felt I had cried through my hurt, they would say, "Well, that's enough crying. There's no need to just keep going on." I would usually dry up after that, then they would pray with us and give us a hug and a kiss. That always brought peace, and we knew our parents loved us.

Proverbs 13:24 says that if you don't correct your children and discipline your children, then you don't love them: **He who spares the rod hates his son, but he who loves him is careful to discipline him** (NIV). My parents loved my brother and me very much. They always expressed their love to us and explained to us that this was the reason they had disciplined us.

Buddy and I disciplined our children in a similar way (except that he did most of the disciplining). Below is an example given by our daughter, Candas, which shows the procedure we followed. We used the same procedure every time. We had to make it clear to our children what they had done wrong if they were to be repentant and correct their ways.

> I remember a spanking, the first one I can remember, that truly caused a change in my behavior and had an impact on me. I was about four years old.
>
> My family was in church, and I was being disrespectful — I must have been talking and moving

around and wiggling. Daddy took me out into the foyer to spank me, but he didn't humiliate me — he waited until the area was perfectly clear. First he explained why I was being spanked — what I had done wrong — then proceeded to spank me.

The spanking hurt my feelings more than it did my bottom. What I remember most is that for the first time I responded correctly. I was truly repentant. I didn't want to do wrong anymore. I went to the bathroom and cried and cried. Daddy didn't let me stay in there too long crying though. My parents let us cry away our hurt, embarrassment and shame. But they didn't let us cry into self-pity either. They could tell from the sound of the crying — it changes and that was why they stopped us.

When I was through crying in the bathroom, Daddy sat me on his knee, and I had to tell him I loved him. We kids hated that part of the discipline because we were so mad at him. But telling him I loved him was instrumental in helping me focus. It kept me from holding grudges and being in bitterness. It made me deal with my emotion and my anger and face it as a fact. Dad always made me face life to show me that there is an advantage to facing things as they come, instead of running and hiding which is my strong natural tendency. He taught me that dealing with things as they come makes life less complicated. Putting things off causes problems to build up and compound. I don't like confrontation.

Then we went over the Scriptures and again talked about what I did wrong and why it was wrong. We looked at what the Bible said about it. I must have heard Ephesians 6:1 a thousand times: **Children, obey your parents in the Lord: for this is right.** I don't remember all of what we talked about because I was still crying some through half of it. But it had a tremendous impact on me. It was truly the establishment of reverence in me.

The rules were very clear. The standards were always set. What was expected of us as far as honoring were the basic Ten Commandments. When we broke them, we knew what was coming — it was no surprise. We knew we were in trouble. There were rules and when we were disobedient, there were consequences to pay. And our parents determined the consequences. My parents point out that children today don't understand authority. We were spanked mostly because we dishonored authority (or because we did something that could have been dangerous).

Some parents think that being consistent in their discipline of their children means spanking their children consistently when they do something wrong. It's true that you should spank your children when you say you will, but "be consistent" means keeping the standards, the rules, the same. Many parents think their kids are being disobedient when it's the parents who are really wrong — they change their standards. They lower or allow the standards to be lowered. I didn't understand this until I was a parent myself. Now it would be the first advice I would give to a new parent.

After I told Daddy I loved him, we prayed. We kids always left with peace. Everybody was fine; everybody was happy. Sometimes we even joked around afterwards. Some of our best jokes were after we were disciplined.

Later on when I had another opportunity to be disrespectful in church, I wasn't. I was filled with the Spirit when I was about five. After the church service, almost everybody cleared out. I was at the altar, but I was facing toward the audience.

There were two little boys talking. One of them I liked, but the other one was mean. As I was praying, I saw the mean little boy whisper and point at me. I knew they were talking about me. I could see that the nice little boy felt kind of bad about doing it, but he laughed too. I thought, "I don't care; I'm with God." I think my reaction was a combination of boldness the Holy Spirit gives to us to witness (Acts 1:8) and the reverence for God that was by then instilled in me. My reverence was a result of that other spanking because I vividly remembered it and that I brought it on myself by being disrespectful in church.

Two of our children have had children, and now, three generations later, that same pattern of discipline is being used to train up their children in the way they should go.

Unfortunately, modern-day "experts" on child raising say that as parents we should sit down and reason with a disobedient child. They say we are just supposed to have a little talk with the child. Then afterward, they say, we should pat him on the head and tell him never to disobey us again.

No wonder so many kids are messed up today after being raised on hogwash like that! The Bible says, **Foolishness is bound in the heart of a child; but the rod of correction shall drive it far from him** (Prov. 22:15).

Discipline Is Not Just Punishment

There is a lot of discussion today about what discipline is and isn't. Some people get discipline confused with punishment, but there is a difference.

Punishment is something you get after the fact. It's only one of the tools of discipline, and it can be an effective one.

Discipline, on the other hand, is instruction and training that will correct your character.

Punishment is what you get when you disobey. You may tell your child, "Don't do thus-and-so." If that child looks you straight in the eye and does it anyway, then it's time for some punishment. As the old saying goes, it's time to "apply the board of education to the seat of wisdom."

Discipline sometimes includes punishment. Sometimes in disciplining your child you need to spank his bottom (never slap his face or hit him anywhere else!), but

71

discipline is much more than just that. Discipline covers every effort a parent makes to teach and train a child — morally, spiritually, mentally and physically — so he will grow up to be a happy, caring adult. That makes it something positive and good.

You also discipline your child by giving him rules and guidelines to follow, by setting an example for him, by putting limits on what he can and cannot do, and by taking away some of his privileges when he disobeys.

For some children this works better than giving them a spanking because the "pain" of the lost privilege lasts longer than the physical pain of a spanking.

Someone may ask, "Do you mean you believe in spanking? Don't you know that's child abuse?"

Yes, we believe in spanking — when it's done in the right way for the right reasons. Disciplining a child with a spanking is scriptural.

> **He that spareth his rod hateth his son: but he that loveth him chasteneth him betimes.**
>
> **Proverbs 13:24**
>
> **Correct thy son, and he shall give thee rest; yea, he shall give delight unto thy soul.**
>
> **Proverbs 29:17**

Most children need a spanking once in a while. But we should never abuse a child — not for any reason. And if discipline isn't done right, it can be abusive.

Some people try to hide abuse of their children behind the old "Spare the rod, spoil the child" saying. But they are in for a big surprise. God is going to deal with them, and they won't get off easy!

In chapter 5 of this book, we saw how Jesus called the little children to Himself so He could bless them. He issued a serious warning to anyone — including parents — who would destroy the spirit, faith and trust of a child. In Matthew 18:5,6 He said:

> **And whoever receives and accepts and welcomes one little child like this for My sake and in My name receives and accepts and welcomes Me.**
>
> **But whoever causes one of these little ones who believe in and acknowledge and cleave to Me to stumble and sin — that is, who entices him, or hinders him in right conduct or thought — it would be better (more expedient and profitable or advan' ʒeouₛ) for him to have a great millstone fastened around his neck and to be sunk in the depth of the sea (AMP).**

Anyone who abuses a child would be better off if he were drowned in the sea than to have to stand before God. Raising children is serious business because we are accountable to God for the way we raise them.

Of course, God will forgive our mistakes if we ask Him. And we will all make mistakes. But human weakness is no excuse for any adult to abuse one of God's little ones.

If you have any doubts about how you are punishing your children — whether you are being abusive — then stop using that form of punishment. If it makes you uncomfortable, don't do it. If you can't spank your children without losing your temper, don't spank them. It's just that simple. Find ways that you are comfortable with and that work for you.

Teach and Train Your Children's Will

The goal of discipline and punishment is not so you can vent your anger or get a load off your chest. It's not to prove that you are the boss.

The goal of discipline is always to help your children grow to become better, more mature and responsible persons. If your kind of discipline is not having that effect, stop doing it and find another way to discipline them.

Many parents get a child's will mixed up with his spirit. As a parent, your goal is not to break your child's spirit but to teach him how to control his will and submit it to the authority of Jesus Christ.

Naturally, the will says, "Me first! My way! I want to do what I want to do!" It is selfish. This is the part of each one of us that we must submit to the will of Jesus Christ.

The spirit is the inner man — who we really are. It's that little child in all of us who is so tender and fragile. Our spirit is wounded when people say cruel things to us and about us.

This is why you as a parent need to be so careful about how you discipline your children. You are trying to shape their will, so you have to be sure that the way you discipline them is re-directing and harnessing their will and not wounding their spirit.

You don't want to do things that will make your children feel bad about who they are. Never call them names or belittle them. Never compare them to anyone else. Never put them down or tell them they are stupid, clumsy, ugly or mean. God says they are of great worth, and nothing they do can change that.

Our job as parents is to teach our kids that *who they are* is fine even when *what they do* is not. Do you see the difference? *Who they are* is their spirit; *what they do* comes from their will.

When you break a child's spirit, he feels unlovable, bad and hopeless. When you re-direct his will, you help him become able to love, to give, to share.

God gave us a will. He could have made us without any will of our own. Then we would have always obeyed Him and done just what He wanted. But He doesn't want us to be a mindless little robot that runs around waiting on Him. He wants us to obey and serve Him because we choose to — because we love Him and want to obey Him.

Our free will is so important to God that He will even let us go to an eternal hell if we choose to.

Now you may say, "Wait a minute. What do you mean, God will let me go to hell? I thought it was God Who sent people to hell."

Absolutely not! God has done everything in His power to keep people out of hell — except take away their free will. He has given us His Word to warn us. He sent His Son, Jesus, Who died to pay the price for our sins. He promised to forgive our sins if we ask Him. And He has given us the Holy Spirit Who empowers us to do right. What more could He do?

No, if someone goes to hell, it's because that person chooses to. God won't send him there. God loves us and doesn't want us to go to hell, but He won't violate our free will and force us to accept Jesus.

This is the kind of discipline we are to use with our children — discipline that teaches them how to control their will and submit it to authority, especially the authority of Jesus Christ.

Discipline Needs Consistency, Fairness and Love

These are the three most important ingredients of good discipline: consistency, fairness and love.

Discipline without consistency is confusing and frightening to a child. He never really knows what is expected of him. From one day to another, the rules change.

So he grows up feeling insecure toward his parents and the world, and he has no respect for rules or authority.

Discipline without fairness is abusive and cruel. Being fair is something parents struggle with daily.

Children have an inborn sense of justice. They know when they have been wronged. When our discipline is too severe for the wrong they have done, we hurt them instead of help them.

We have to make the punishment fit the child. What works for one child may be totally wrong for another.

As an example, one couple we heard about have three children. The first two were typical kids when they were little. They got into trouble like all kids do, and a spanking or two was all it took to discipline them and set them on the right road.

Then their third child was born. This little boy had a strong will. They tried all the same things to discipline him, but nothing seemed to work. Even spanking him didn't work. It only made him more determined to have his own way.

They tried everything they knew to discipline him before they finally found out what worked. By simply being told how disappointed they were in his actions and being made to go to his room, the boy was quickly reduced to tears and true repentance.

As we read in a previous chapter, Proverbs 22:6 from *The Amplified Bible* says, **Train up a child in the way he should go [and in keeping with his individual gift or bent], and when he is old he will not depart from it.** Your child's bent is his uniqueness, his personality, his special talents. It's the thing that makes him different from every other child. So we are to train our children according to their individuality.

Some kids are as tender and fragile as young plants. They can be easily bruised or even broken. And once the damage is done, it can't be undone. The smallest harsh word from Mom or Dad will break their hearts.

When you discipline this kind of child, you have to use a lot of sensitivity and tenderness.

Still other kids seem to be born wearing combat boots. You can talk to them, yell at them, spank them, and do everything you know to do, and still you wonder if it's making any difference. With these kids it takes some special time and effort to discover the best ways to discipline them.

Most children are somewhere in the middle. They have their good days and bad days. The key to knowing how to discipline them is in knowing them and spending time with them.

It's hard for parents to be fair all the time. In fact, it's almost impossible, but we have to try. This is why it's so important that we really know our kids. They are all different and they all change. What works best for one may not work with another. What is good for one may be harmful to another. What works for a child at one age may not work at another age.

The third ingredient of good discipline is love — the most important of all.

By disciplining without love, you are simply taking out your frustration and anger on your kids instead of doing what is best for them. Never discipline a child when you are angry or out of control. Even if that child has done wrong, disciplining him in anger will be doing more harm than good. Wait until you cool off before trying to deal with the situation.

God's Word says:

And, ye fathers, provoke not your children to wrath: but bring them up in the nurture and admonition of the Lord.

Ephesians 6:4

Look at this verse in *The Amplified Bible*:

Fathers, do not irritate and provoke your children to anger — do not exasperate them to resentment — but rear them [tenderly] in the training and discipline and the counsel and admonition of the Lord.

This is the kind of discipline every parent should use. We must be consistent and fair in our discipline, and we must always discipline in love. We must do what the last part of this verse tells us to do: rear our children in the training and discipline of the Lord.

The Importance of Teaching and Training

So many times, people fail to realize that there is a difference between teaching their children and training them.

You teach your children when you tell them right from wrong. You instill in them what the Bible says. You teach them that they are under your authority and, ultimately, under God's authority. And you try to live an example before them.

You are training your children when you help them do what is right: obeying you and God. To train them means to mold their character. This is what God wants us to do with our children.

You are training your children when you require them to obey you and do what you have taught them. Small kids, especially, don't have enough self-discipline to make themselves do what they know they are supposed to do, so you have to make them do it.

But as a child grows older and his will becomes more controllable, he starts choosing to do right. You don't have to make him obey as much. He obeys because he has been trained. As he grows spiritually, he will also learn to obey God more. The Holy Spirit will work in him, helping him to control his actions and develop spiritual fruit.

Usually, teaching and training go together. For instance, you may say to your son: "Johnny, I want you to straighten up your room. So make your bed, hang up your clothes and put your toys away. It's important that you learn how to take care of your things."

Now, eight-year-old little Johnny should be able to handle that assignment without any problem. But his will is sometimes lazy, and it's hard for him to control. He would rather watch TV than clean up his room. So you may have to make him obey.

You say, "Johnny, I expect you to obey me and straighten up your room within the next hour. If you do...." Then you tell him what the consequences of his obedience will be: he can watch his favorite TV show, go outside and play with his friends or invite a friend over to spend the night.

"But if you don't do as I ask...." Then you tell him what will happen if he fails to obey you: he won't be allowed to watch TV until he cleans his room, he will spend the evening sitting on his bed or he will be denied some special privilege.

By following through with your actions, you are not only teaching your son that he needs to have a clean room and take care of his things, but you are training him to do that. Hopefully, by the time he is grown, he will have a good understanding of the value of his possessions, and he will take care of both his things and other people's things.

You are also teaching and training him what it means to be a good steward of all that God has given us. Being a good steward involves not only things, but it also includes taking care of your own spirit, soul and body. Ultimately, you are responsible for what you do with your spirit. You are responsible for what you do with your mind, will and emotions. And you are responsible for what you do with your body.

If your children don't understand stewardship in its totality, just being a steward over things won't help them choose to do right in all areas. You can help them to become a good steward of what God has given them by training them to brush their teeth, to do their homework and to pray before eating dinner. By your own example, you can reinforce what it means to be a good steward.

While you are working on the outside, teaching and training your child, God is working on the inside, changing his heart. God is teaching and training him to do right — not because he will get into trouble if he doesn't, but because it's the best thing for him to do.

You can tell your kids to do something until you are blue in the face, but until you add training to it, you aren't doing yourself or them much good. Your kids need both teaching and training.

Spend Time Together

It's vitally important that you spend time with your children if you expect to do a good job teaching and training them. You have to preach the truth, and you have to practice what you preach if they are to respect you and listen to you.

So many people have the mistaken idea that they can give their kids the time and attention they need by spending a few minutes with them each day. They say, "I may not have a lot of time to spend with them, but what we do spend together is quality time."

Exactly where did this "quality time" idea get started? Quality time with your kids isn't better than quantity time. It may be better than no time at all, but kids need more than a few minutes thrown at them each day.

Suppose you go into a fancy restaurant. You are really hungry, so you order a steak. But the waiter comes out with a little steak about two inches wide, two inches long and an inch thick. And then he gives you a bill for $50.

"What!" you shout. "Fifty dollars for a tiny piece of steak like that? But I'm still hungry! I need a bigger steak than that."

"But, sir," the waiter says, "this is quality steak. There may not be much of it, but it's the best steak we have."

How would you feel in a situation like that? Cheated? Angry? Unimportant?

That's how our children feel when we give them a few minutes of quality time instead of the time and attention they really need and want.

Yes, it's hard. Sometimes it means we can't do the things we want or even need to do. But most things will wait — kids don't. They grow up so quickly! And then all the opportunities you had to teach and train them to serve God are gone.

Many times parents have looked back over their lives and seen how they missed it. Their hearts are breaking, so they say something like this: "I'd give anything to have my little child back again. There were so many things I meant to teach him, so many things I should have done with him. I meant to teach him about Jesus and read the Bible to him. I meant to take him to church. But I never seemed to find the time. I was always too busy. And now he's grown."

Parent, your children need you now! Don't wait until it's too late. Their teaching and training is a day-by-day job

81

that can't be put off. They won't wait until you are free to spend time with them. If you don't teach and train them, someone or something else will. It may be the television, or their friends or the gang that hangs out down on the corner. But they will learn from someone. Make sure they learn God's will and plan for their lives through you.

What kind of friendship or marriage could you have with someone if you never spent time with him, talked with him and shared with him?

Yet we expect to know and understand our children and have them to know and understand us even when we have spent only a few minutes with them each day. No wonder we have a generation gap.

Parents must have real communication with their kids. There must be time spent talking with them, not just giving them orders or disciplining them. That's a sin!

Dads are supposed to be the spiritual leaders of our homes. How can we teach and train our children if we only spend a minute or two a day talking with them?

Our churches are full of "Sunday widows and orphans" — women and children who go to church without their men because the men are "too busy" to go. When the kids are little, Mom can usually get them to go to church. But when they become teenagers, forget it! Why should the kids go to church when Dad stays home?

Men who have shirked their God-given responsibilities and let their wives be the spiritual leader of the home will be held accountable before God. If a dad (or a mom) doesn't take the kids to church and spiritually teach and train them, he's hindering their spiritual development.

You may say, "Aren't you being a little hard on parents? Some have to work on Sunday, and others only get that one day off a week to rest."

If we are being hard, it's only because the stakes are so high. The eternal souls of your children are at risk. We want you to understand how important your job as a parent is, and we want to inspire you to do the best you can. That's all God requires of you.

Ultimately, whether your children serve God is their decision, but you have to do all you can to help them choose Him. *And the time to start is now!*

There is an old saying that goes: "As the twig is bent, so grows the tree." This, in a nutshell, is the secret of good discipline. When your children are young, you have to start bending those "twigs" toward God, and keep working on it every day.

Spend time with your children. Play with them. Pray with them. Teach and train them. Keep on bending those little twigs until one day the trees are big and beautiful and reaching for the heavens!

8

Help Your Teenagers Cope

There is a story we have heard about an oil well fire that was out of control. The owner tried every way he could to get the fire put out, but nothing worked. Then he offered $10,000 to anyone who could get the job done.

One by one, different groups of firemen from local towns showed up and did their best to fight the fire. But, still, nothing seemed to work.

Then one day three men from another little town nearby came to the rescue. Their fire truck was 40 years old, and they didn't have much equipment to use to fight the fire, but that didn't seem to stop them. They drove out to that oil rig with their siren screaming and red lights flashing. Then the truck just kept circling around the oil well, while the men stood there throwing sand and water at the fire. But they managed to put it out!

When the owner handed them his $10,000 check, he asked what they planned to do with the money.

Immediately, one of them said, "Well, first we're going to get some brakes for our fire truck!"

Being a Teenager Is Hard

That story is a perfect picture of adolescence. A teenager is like a fire truck with no brakes. Everything is out of control. He races through life with lights flashing and sirens screaming, while Mom and Dad are standing on the sidelines and trying to put out the fire with a sack of sand and a bucket of water.

Now it's easy for adults to forget how hard it is being a teenager. When a child reaches those years, his whole life changes. Suddenly, his parents expect him to act like an adult, while his body is going through all kinds of changes. Emotionally, he's up one minute and down the next.

Growing up can be as difficult and painful as trying to climb a mountain with your bare hands. A teenager is changing in so many ways. Within a few years, he has to make some decisions for his life like: *Where am I going? What will I do? What do I really believe?* In other words, he's becoming an adult.

At no other time in life are there as many challenges and changes as during teenage years. It's like being in an earthquake. When the ground starts moving under your feet, there is no safe place you can run — unless you are a teenager who has been raised in a Christian home by loving and involved parents.

That young person has something to hang on to, something that will keep him through the times ahead. God will always be there with him. This is the message of hope and encouragement we can give our kids as they enter adolescence.

You see, God loves young people.

The Bible is full of stories about young people who were used of God in marvelous ways. David was just a teenager when he slew Goliath. Joseph was only a young man when he was taken away as a slave into Egypt. Daniel was young when the children of Israel were carried into Babylon by King Nebuchadnezzar. But he was willing to serve God no matter what. Because of his commitment, he was used by God as a tremendous witness and testimony to God's power.

Young people have the drive, the energy and the vision to do some wonderful things. That's part of the reason God loves to use them. That's also why Satan wants them. He wants to harness that energy for himself. And that's why the world offers so many distractions to young people.

Satan knows if he can get our kids while they are young, it will be harder for them to break free from the world. He throws all kinds of things at them trying to win them over. He uses anything and everything he can — like peer pressure, sex, the need for acceptance, a drive for independence — to destroy their lives and bring them into bondage to sin. When our kids are at their weakest, Satan's attacks are strongest.

That's why as parents we have to work harder to protect our kids from those satanic attacks when they reach their teens. We have to pray harder, listen more, love more, and trust God more to bring them through.

Now, don't get us wrong. We aren't saying that all the things teenagers go through are necessarily of the devil (although that thought probably does cross the minds of most teens' parents). No, the changes and feelings of confusion that young people go through are a normal part of growing up. It's just that Satan often uses these things to draw them away. He wants to separate them from the Church and from their families. He tries to replace the standards and beliefs they were raised with. But, most important, he wants to keep them away from God.

Teenagers are so vulnerable, and the devil is so crafty. Even though they were raised in strong Christian homes, were taught the Bible and know who they are in Jesus Christ, they still can suffer from self-doubt and confusion during those years. And children who enter adolescence without a firm foundation in Him are almost sure to be shipwrecked.

Being a teenager today is tough business. Many of them feel self-conscious and clumsy and full of fear. They can be overwhelmed by circumstances around them. Yet they are bombarded by a society that says for them to feel loved and accepted they have to be beautiful, sexy and cool. They want so much to be independent, self-confident and in complete control of their lives.

They feel like no one in the world understands how they feel and what they are going through. They don't realize that other teens feel the same way they do and that every adult was once a teenager, too. They also forget that the things they are going through are only temporary. No one is a teenager forever. It only feels like forever!

Help Your Teens Learn To Thrive

So how do we as Christian parents help our teens not only survive but thrive during these days? We can't give you a simple guide to get you through everything you will face as a parent, but we can share some principles and pointers that will help.

We have already talked about some of these things in previous chapters, but let's go over them again to remind you of how important they are.

1. Pray for Your Children Every Day

Prayer is one of the most powerful tools at your disposal for fighting the devil on behalf of your children. Prayer makes a difference! God can do the impossible — and He will — when we pray.

2. Love Your Teenagers Unconditionally

That means you need to love them no matter what — and tell them you love them every day. You won't always like what they do or how they act (and you can tell them that you don't!), but you still love them. And nothing they do or don't do will change that.

It's important that your kids — whatever their age — know there is a difference between what they do (their will) and what they are (their spirit). They can control what they do, but they can't help what they are. If they think your love is based on what they do, they will always be working to win your love. Unfortunately, they will never feel that they have earned it.

Many parents make the mistake of comparing a child's conduct with the child's person. If Mary does what her mother wants, she's a "good girl," and Mother loves her. But if she disobeys, she's a "bad girl," and no one loves a bad person. It doesn't take Mary long to figure out that she will only be loved if she does all the right things. And since no child — or adult for that matter — is perfect, Mary feels like a failure. She feels unlovable and bad.

One woman who grew up with this kind of thinking explained it this way:

"I always felt that somewhere there was a line, and if I ever stepped over that line, that was it for me. I had gone too far. I had been too bad. My parents wouldn't love me anymore, and even God would wash His hands of me. I would be without hope.

"Unfortunately, I didn't know where that line was. Every time I failed or made a mistake or sinned, I was terrified that maybe I had crossed that line. So I determined to try harder. I would try to be perfect, but I kept making mistakes.

"Finally, I realized it was futile. I couldn't be perfect. I could never do enough to make myself into a good person. So I lost hope. I got angry at my parents, at God and at the world. I was competing in a game I could never win, because I could never be good enough to deserve their love."

That's not how life is supposed to be. As parents, we should teach our children that there is a big difference between what they do and who they really are. We love them for one reason: because they are our kids. And that will never change!

It's not easy to love like that. It's not easy to keep loving a child who constantly disobeys you and rebels against you. But real love is more than a feeling. It's a decision and a commitment to do what is best for your child, no matter how you feel, or what it costs or how much it hurts. That's a real sacrificial love — the kind of love God has for us.

> For scarcely for a righteous man will one die: yet peradventure for a good man some would even dare to die.
>
> But God commendeth his love toward us, in that, while we were yet sinners, Christ died for us.
>
> Romans 5:7,8

God loved us even before we knew Him or loved Him. He loved us even though we had done nothing to deserve His love. He loved us so much that it cost Him the life of His only Son on the cross at Calvary.

> For by grace are ye saved through faith; and that not of yourselves: it is the gift of God:
>
> Not of works, lest any man should boast.
>
> Ephesians 2:8,9

God loves us simply because we are His creation, and nothing can ever change that. We don't have to earn His love — we can't! We try to do good simply because we want to please the One Who loves us so much.

Always make it clear to your teenager that while he may be acting in an unacceptable way, he's still deeply loved. He has personal worth that is unchanged by what he does. He's of value and is loved simply because he's your child and God's child.

This is especially important for teenagers. They feel so pressured to compete, perform and succeed. The world says that money, looks, brains and ability are what gives them personal worth, and teenagers feel that they are lacking in most, if not all, of these areas. But the world is wrong! Its standards are false and unfair, and we have to help our teenagers understand this.

If they feel that they are unconditionally loved at home and by God, they will be better able to cope with a world that judges them unfairly.

3. Keep the Lines of Communication Open

Real communication is both talking and listening. It's listening to what your kids are saying and to what they aren't saying. Communication is finding out what they really think, feel and believe, even when it is different from what you think, feel and believe. Let them see you as a parent who struggles, who doubts and who has to deal with fear.

When your children are in the mood to talk, stop what you are doing and truly listen to them. Don't give advice — and don't interrupt — just listen. When you feel the time is right, ask questions about their feelings. This way they will tell you what they really think and feel without fear of rejection. And whatever you do, avoid accusations. That will immediately shut and lock the door to any honest sharing.

Heart-to-heart communication doesn't just happen. Sometimes you have to prime the pump by creating an atmosphere for it. Popping popcorn, making candy, or playing a game together may give you a perfect opportunity for really talking with your teenager.

The desire to communicate comes from God. According to Genesis, chapters 1-3, God created Adam and Eve for fellowship and communication. Each day God would come down to walk and talk with them.

Communication begins when your kids are born, and it grows as you spend time together. You should never outgrow the need and desire to communicate with each other.

Unfortunately, most of us get so busy with life that we stop communicating and sharing. When our kids become teenagers, there are lots of things — school, ball practice, music lessons, work, dating — to keep them so busy that it seems there's never time to talk. But during their teen years, more than ever, they need for us to keep the lines of communication open.

Many teenagers go through a stage where they withdraw from their families. They spend their time at home in their bedrooms with the doors closed. Parents feel shut out, and suddenly they don't know their own kids anymore.

If your child refuses to talk, you can't force him to, but you can set limits on how much time he spends alone in his room or with his friends. Insist that your family has at least one meal together each day. During that time, don't talk about problems. Just try to enjoy each other's company.

In our opinion, it isn't a good idea for a child to have a television set in his room. It could keep the parent from knowing what he's watching or for how long. It's better to use TV viewing as something the family does together.

A teenager needs time to be alone, and you should respect that. But you have the right to expect him to do certain things, like help around the house, join in family activities whenever possible, go to church with you and do his homework.

Most important, let your teenager know you are there for him, to talk or to listen. Remind him from time to time that you are available to talk and pray with him whenever he is ready. Be willing to talk about anything he wants to talk about, and respect his opinions even if you don't agree with them.

4. Give Your Teenagers the Independence They Earn

As your teenagers get older, their need for independence gets greater. And that's the way God meant for it to be. God didn't intend for your kids to be dependent upon you for the rest of their lives.

There is a natural progression of things: first, children are born dependent on their parents, then they grow up and become independent. It's a gradual, day-by-day process.

When your children hit their teen years, they start to become more and more independent. They want to pick out their own clothes and wear their hair the way they like it. They want to choose their own friends. They want to do whatever they want to do, whenever they want to do it.

If you have been working on a strong Christian foundation in your kids' lives, by the time they get to this point, they probably already know what they can and cannot do, and why. If they have proven themselves to be trustworthy, you know you can give them greater independence. If not, you have to hold off on their independence until they are ready for it.

That's the challenge: knowing when a child is ready for independence and how much, and protecting him from things he isn't ready for. At the same time, you have to protect the rights of other members of the family. And that's a pretty big order!

Back during the Depression, people didn't worry so much about personal independence. There wasn't a lot of "teenage rebellion" as we know it today. Most young people were too busy helping their folks keep food on the table and a roof over their heads. In those days they didn't have a lot of choices. Kids became independent whether they were ready for it or not.

Things are different now. Teenagers today usually don't have to work to help their families make ends meet. But they have to make some choices, and knowing how to make the right choice to succeed can be tough. The consequences of making wrong choices can also be tough. Most teenagers these days want their independence, but are terrified of it at the same time. That's why they need the wisdom and guidance of their parents during this time.

5. Learn To Forgive and Forget, and Always Expect the Best

One of the best ways to help your teenagers thrive is to forgive and forget, and to always expect the best of them. Plenty of opportunities will come along for you to say to them, *I told you so!* But when you feel it coming on, just bite your tongue. The last thing they need is a smug parent rubbing their nose in their mistake. What they really need and want is for you to forgive and forget their failure and to keep believing in them in spite of it.

Remember the story of the Prodigal Son in Luke 15? That boy really messed up his life. He demanded his inheritance, then he went off and spent it all. He had been a fool, doing everything his father had taught him not to do. When he came home with his tail between his legs, his father didn't lecture him or even say, "I told you so." No, the father forgave him and forgot it.

That's the way God treats us, and that's the way we should treat our children. No matter how many times they fail, we must forgive them and forget their wrong. We have to keep believing that, in spite of the past, they will do better the next time. Remember First Corinthians 13:7,8 says, love ...**beareth all things, believeth all things, hopeth all things, endureth all things.** [Love] **never faileth.**

When you forgive and forget your children's mistakes, you give them a powerful example of God's grace toward us.

6. Spend As Much Time With Your Teenagers As Possible

We have shared about the importance of spending time together, but it's worth mentioning again. It's hard to spend time with your teenagers. For one thing, they would probably rather be with their friends than with an old fogey like you, but you still need to spend time together. You can teach them things they will never learn from their friends.

Try to spend some time alone with them each week. Go out to eat. Go shopping. Play a game together. Do whatever they want to do. When you take time to be with them, you are saying to them, "You're important to me." You are making yourself available to talk, and you are spending time just getting to know each other. That's important!

7. Keep God in the Picture

When your kids become teens, it's vitally important that you keep taking them to church, keep having family devotions, keep praying with them and reading the Word of God with them. It will probably be harder to keep your teenagers interested in the things of God, but keep on doing what you have been doing.

Unfortunately, some people tend to think that God can't use young people, but He can and He will. It's our job to provide our teenagers with opportunities to minister. Through our example we can help them by showing them how God uses us. When you go out witnessing, take them with you. Let them see you pray for someone or lead a devotion. Let them be a part of your ministry, then you can encourage and guide them in the ministry God gives them, and they will want to serve the Lord rather than rebel against Him.

So many times preachers' kids who have grown up in the house of God later rebel and turn away from the things of the Lord. When this happens, it really hurts, but God is always there to walk with us through it. Although our children didn't rebel, that doesn't mean that they didn't get into trouble every now and then. They, like most kids, were curious and were faced with the temptation to experiment and do something crazy like drink too much once just to see what it was like. Their motive, however, was more out of curiousity than rebellion. They were saying, "Hey, is this a good thing?" as opposed to, "I'm doing this to get back at you."

If we were to single out one thing we did in raising our children that kept them from this rebellious attitude, it would be that we drilled into them at a young age a respect for authority. That meant that they should respect their parents just as the Scripture says in Ephesians 6:1,2. As a matter of fact, disrespect for parents, or for any authority, was the number one reason for giving them a spanking.

As our children reached their teenage years, this same respect for authority transferred on over into their relationship with God. He was becoming the authority in their life, and what He said went. One of our daughters told us recently that she had always been afraid to rebel because she had learned a reverence for God at such a young age. Developing this kind of reverential fear of God in our children will help to keep them from rebelling against the things of the Lord.

As children grow into teenagers and become more independent, both physically and emotionally, they will also be growing stronger and more independent spiritually. They won't need you to tell them right from wrong, and they will depend more and more on God for guidance as they grow into the ministry God has prepared for them.

Other Ways You Can Help

Be Understanding

Remember how you felt as a teenager. Be sympathetic to your children's problems and struggles, and support them through everything. In other words, be on their side.

Be Patient

Just remember: teenage years won't last forever, and they can be a time of growth for your whole family. When the going gets tough, remind yourself that you were a teenager once — and you survived. Your children will survive, too. Keep focusing on the good things, the little things that make life better.

Get Help

If you feel your children's problems are more than you can handle, *get help.* Talk with your minister, or a Christian counselor or another parent who has experienced the same problem you are facing.

Many families suffer in silence. They don't want anyone to know that they are having problems. But Galatians 6:2 says, **Bear ye one another's burdens, and so fulfil the law of Christ.** We all have problems and we need each other. So don't be afraid to reach out to someone who can help you and your family.

Teenage years can be difficult, but they can also be wonderful as you, the parent, see the good seeds you have sown in your children begin to take root and grow. This is the time when your kids become adults and your job as a parent ends. Someone once described a parent as the only person who truly succeeds when he has worked himself out of a job. That's true!

9

Teach Your Children About Sex

Sex!

Just say the word and parents get nervous.

There is the story of the little girl who came home from school one day and asked her mother, "Mama, where did I come from?"

Immediately the mother's heart jumped up to her throat! In her mind, that big day had finally come when she would have to tell her daughter about the facts of life. So she started at the beginning.

After a few minutes, the girl interrupted and said, "No, Mama, that's not what I mean. My friend said she came from Minnesota, and I was just wondering where I came from."

Parents who can talk to their kids about anything else get embarrassed when the subject of sex comes up. Why is this? Maybe it's because our parents and grandparents seemed to feel that sex was dirty and that "nice people" — especially Christians! — didn't openly discuss sex. But this isn't true.

The Biblical View of Sex

God invented sex. The world and the devil had no part in it. Sex is God's gift to a man and woman who are joined in holy matrimony. It's the bonding that makes two people become one. The unity of the marriage relationship is symbolic of the union of Jesus Christ and His Bride, the Church. (Eph. 5:22-33.)

When God created Adam and Eve, He commanded them to be fruitful and multiply. (Gen. 1:26-28.) The apostle Paul said, **Marriage is honourable in all, and the bed undefiled: but whoremongers and adulterers God will judge** (Heb. 13:4).

God never intended for sex to be misused and made vulgar as it is in our society today. He intended for sex to be a beautiful and joyous act of love between a husband and his wife.

Sex was not designed by God for use between just any man and woman. God's Word teaches that sex outside of marriage is wrong and that those who indulge in it will suffer some grave consequences. Let's look at this in the writings of the apostle Paul:

> **Know ye not that the unrighteous shall not inherit the kingdom of God? Be not deceived: neither fornicators, nor idolaters, nor adulterers, nor effeminate, nor abusers of themselves with mankind [homosexuals],**
>
> **Nor thieves, nor covetous, nor drunkards, nor revilers, nor extortioners, shall inherit the kingdom of God.**
>
> **And such were some of you: but ye are washed, but ye are sanctified, but ye are justified in the name of the Lord Jesus, and by the Spirit of our God.**
>
> **1 Corinthians 6:9-11**

The World's View of Sex

Christian parents have their work cut out for them today when it comes to sex education. It isn't easy to teach biblical sexual behavior to children who live in a sexually permissive society.

Even kids from the best of Christian homes are bombarded with permissive, often explicit, sex.

Everywhere they look, they see it on TV, in movies, in books and magazines, on billboards. They are lambasted with the message: "It's okay to have sex anytime — whenever, wherever, whatever way you choose." And anyone who disagrees with this is thought to be old-fashioned and out of step with the modern world.

In his book, *The Hex of Modern Day Sex*,[1] Evangelist Lowell Lundstrom states:

"It's difficult — if not impossible — for susceptible teenagers to resist the message of free sex that society so blatantly proclaims. Young people are at a vulnerable time in their maturation when they desperately want to be loved, accepted and approved by others, particularly by their peers. Under these conditions, they are easy prey for the false promises free sex offers.

"'If you love me, you'll go all the way.'

"'All the popular kids have sex.'

"'No one is a virgin anymore.'

"'Prove you're a man and not a wimp.'

"'Teenagers get the message in a hurry that they can find love, acceptance, approval and happiness by having sex."

The tragedy is that once young people believe Satan's lies and fall into his sex trap, they suffer the loss of self-respect and innocence that they can never regain.

During one television interview, a beautiful teenage girl told how she was pressured by her friends to lose her virginity. So she did, thinking it would make her more acceptable in her gang. After she had given in to sex, she found that those "friends" acted differently toward her.

---

[1](Sisseton, South Dakota, 1985), p. 23.

Having once made fun of her for being a virgin, they suddenly rejected her, calling her "a slut."

Kids these days appear to be sex-wise, but they still struggle with the age-old double standard: boys are "expected" to have sex — or at least try to — while girls are supposed to be "nice" and always be the ones to set the limits and save their virginity for marriage.

It seems that young people today are having sex at earlier ages. They are more sexually active than any previous generation. And, as a result, more teenage girls are becoming pregnant.[2]

These situations are enough to bring fear into the hearts of Christian parents. We can't take things for granted these days. Just because our children were "brought up right" and taken to Sunday school and church does not mean they will automatically make responsible decisions regarding their sexual behavior. So from the earliest years, we parents need to discuss sex openly and honestly with our kids.

Start Sex Education Early

Sex education should begin in the home as early as a child begins to ask questions. You should answer questions about the differences between boys and girls and how babies are born just as freely and matter-of-factly as you would any other question your child might ask.

There are some beautifully illustrated books available in Christian bookstores to help you teach your small children the basics of sex education from a Christian perspective. You can sit down with your child at storybook time and read these picture books together. Then reinforce the story with your own spiritual instruction regarding sex.

---

[2]Richard M. Lerner, Ann C. Peterson, and Jeanne Brooks-Gunn, *Encyclopedia of Adolescence*, 2 vols. (New York: Garland Publishing, 1991), 2:1031.

Christian author Bruce Narramore says in his book, *Parenting With Love and Limits*[3]:

". . . sex education should be a normal part of daily living. If we relegate it to specific times or to books and lectures, we misunderstand our task. Sex education isn't a lecture or a few bits of information. It's a way of life. Just as information about sex and attitudes toward sex are woven throughout Scripture, our children's sex education should unfold naturally in our daily interaction with them."

Be honest in the way you handle your young children's questions and feelings. Your attitude toward their interest in their bodies and sexuality will help them develop a responsible and healthy view of sex.

Children can't comprehend all the facts of life at one sitting. When they ask you a question about sex, don't try to tell them everything at once. But it's good when you can use day-to-day events that happen as examples of life — things like the birth of a kitten or puppy, or a trip to the zoo where animals are seen with their young. That will encourage questions and teach your kids about sexual behavior.

Discuss sex along the way as your children can receive it. The main thing is that you be sensitive to their curiosity about the subject.

Parents who wait for the right time to discuss sex with their kids may wait until it's too late. Studies have shown that young girls are at the greatest risk of becoming pregnant during the first few months of their sexual activity.[4]

---

[3]Taken from the book, *Parenting With Love and Limits* by Bruce Narramore. Copyright © 1979 by Bruce Narramore. Used by permission of Zondervan Publishing House.

[4]Richard M. Lerner, Ann C. Peterson, and Jeanne Brooks-Gunn, *Encyclopedia of Adolescence*, 2 vols. (New York: Garland Publishing, 1991), 1:176.

Some parents think that sex education consists of sitting down one day and warning their kids about what could happen by saying something like: "Son, there's the danger of venereal diseases!" or "Daughter, you could get pregnant!"

But sex education involves much more than that.

Your Attitude About Sex Is Catching

Positive sex education begins with parents who have a wholesome attitude toward their own bodies and sexuality. Do you and your spouse openly show affection at home in front of your kids? Parents communicate some powerful unspoken messages about sex in their relationship with one another.

Love and affection are not something a husband and wife should be ashamed of or embarrassed about. In His Word, through the Song of Solomon, God Himself teaches us the intimacies of lovemaking between a married couple in love. All married couples should read this book from time to time.

A positive example by parents can give their children an understanding of the total relationship between men and women. Usually, a son responds to his wife the same way he saw his father respond to his mother — and vice versa for a daughter. If the father views women as dumb and inferior, the son will probably carry that same image of women into his own marriage relationship. Similarly, if the daughter is taught that sex is dirty and that men use women as sex objects, she will have a hard time with her own marital relationship.

We believe that when parents have a healthy attitude about their own bodies and their own sexuality, that same kind of attitude will be passed on to their children.

God Prohibits Sex Outside of Marriage

When it comes to the subject of sex before marriage, don't just tell your kids they can't do it; teach them why. They need to know what God's Word teaches about sex and the consequences of disobedience. The Bible says we are sinning against our own bodies when we have sex outside of marriage. (1 Cor. 6:18.)

The apostle Paul wrote these words to the Corinthian church:

> ...The body is not intended for sexual immorality, but [is intended] for the Lord, and the Lord [is intended] for the body [to save, sanctify and raise it again].
>
> Do you not see and know that your bodies are members (bodily parts) of Christ, the Messiah? Am I therefore to take the parts of Christ and make [them] parts of a prostitute? Never! Never!
>
> Or do you not know and realize that when a man joins himself to a prostitute he becomes one body with her? The two, it is written, shall become one flesh.
>
> But the person who is united to the Lord becomes one person with Him.
>
> Shun immorality and all sexual looseness — flee from impurity [in thought, word or deed]. Any other sin which a man commits is one outside the body, but he who commits sexual immorality sins against his own body.
>
> Do you not know that your body is the temple — the very sanctuary — of the Holy Spirit Who lives within you, Whom you have received [as a Gift] from God? You are not your own.
>
> You were bought for a price — purchased with a preciousness and paid for, made His own. So then, honor God and bring glory to Him in your body.
>
> **1 Corinthians 6:13,15-20 AMP**

The Bible says that a man and woman, who are committed to each other by marriage and bonded together by sexual love, become one flesh. (Gen. 2:24.) They symbolize the image of God. This is God's divine plan for sex. No matter how the world tries to dress it up or defend it, sex outside of marriage is a sin and carries with it the penalty of sin. Your children need to know this.

You must teach your kids that sex can't be separated from responsibility. There's no such thing as "free sex" or sex without strings.

Unfortunately, television and movies are the biggest pushers of free sex. Some of the most popular TV programs are those with "live-in" plots. Couples meet and jump into bed on the first date. The message is loud and clear: sex is fun for everyone, and when it stops being fun, it's time to end that relationship and go to another.

One teenager asked, "Why is the Bible so full of 'Thou shalt nots'? It seems like God is against everything that's fun or enjoyable!"

God isn't against our fun; He is for our good. When He said, **Thou shalt not...**, it was for our protection. God is not a spoilsport. When He said, **Thou shalt not steal**, it was to teach us how to respect the rights of others. He said, **Thou shalt not lie**, because it's what comes out of us that either defiles us or honors us.

God's laws concerning sin are for our protection and benefit. When He said, **Thou shalt not commit adultery**, He wasn't trying to deprive us of pleasure; He was looking out for our highest good. He wants us to escape the misery and heartbreak we will surely have if we fail to follow His plan for our happiness.

No one buys a brand-new car and then tries to take it for a spin across the lake. We all know that a car wasn't made to float on water like a boat. And people don't go around complaining because they can't drive their cars across the lake.

By the same token, God designed and made us to have sex only in marriage. That's what the Bible says, and anything else is not what God intended. We are only hurting ourselves when we go against God's original plan and intent.

Keep Your Children Involved in Church

So how can you help your children counteract the world's peer pressure?

One of the most positive ways is by participating in a Bible-believing church. Young people who are actively involved in this kind of church have a distinct advantage over kids who don't attend church.

Children usually choose their friends from the kids they associate with in their neighborhoods, at school and at church. If you take your children to church, they are much more likely to choose friends from church who are good for them.

Attend church regularly and encourage your kids to participate in the youth activities. Be involved with the youth of your church. Help by providing them with fun things to do. There needs to be some uplifting activities that are alternatives to the kinds of activities the world offers them.

Of course, attending church doesn't guarantee that your kids will choose the right kind of friends or that they will always make the right decisions about their sexuality. But the odds of their doing so are much better if they are sitting under the influence of God's Word in a church that upholds them with prayer and encouragement. When they have been taught the Word of God, they are better equipped to make the kind of decisions that will be right for them and for the people who love them.

Know Your Children's Friends

Of course, not all of the young people who attend church are Christians. Sometimes the worst kids in school are the ones from church. That's why it's so important that you know your children's friends. The friends they choose can make a tremendous difference in their lives.

During their teen years, the peer pressure your kids face is staggering. The people they hang around with can have a great deal of influence on what they do, so you need to know the people your kids are spending a large amount of their time with.

Get to know who your children's friends are. Get acquainted with them. Invite them to your house for a meal, or have them join your family on an outing. Find out about them. How do they act? What do they believe? What are their ambitions in life? Know what kind of influence they are having on your kids.

The Bible says, **Do not be so deceived and misled! Evil companionships, (communion, associations) corrupt and deprave good manners and morals and character** (1 Cor. 15:33 AMP). When parents stand by and allow their children to run around with kids who have a bad influence on them, they are being irresponsible, and they will reap the results. Many young people are strong, stable men and women of God today because their parents refused to let them associate with undesirable friends.

Christian young people can be a great encouragement to one another. When they run into problems, there is someone their own age they can talk to and pray with. They can share the same activities and live according to biblical standards. They can withstand the world's peer pressure together.

Stay Open to Your Children

Your children need you as much when they are teenagers as they did when they were toddlers. The only thing that changes is the kind of needs they have as they grow up. So it's absolutely essential that you keep the lines of communication open. Listen to them with love and understanding.

Parents make a serious mistake by assuming that because their kids see and hear so much about sex today they already know everything about the subject. But just having information doesn't mean it's correct or that they understand it.

When your kids have a question about something they don't understand, they should feel free to come and talk with you about it. And they will — as long as they know you won't make them feel guilty for being curious about life and sex. By building this kind of understanding, you will from time to time hear them knocking on your door just to talk.

On the other hand, suppose your kids come to you with a question about sex, and immediately you begin to act suspicious and start giving them a lecture on morality. If you make them feel like they are committing a sin by even asking such questions, they won't make that mistake twice. They will quit coming to you about it, and they will find somebody else to talk to who won't embarrass them.

No matter how shocking or disturbing your children's questions may be, you need to be calm. You should act in a matter-of-fact manner. (Think back to the way you felt when you were asking about sex.) Just say something like this: "That's a good question. I'm glad you asked it." Then take it from there.

Now you may wonder, "Why can't I just let my kids learn things like that in sex education classes at school?"

Because schools teach children only the physiological facts of life. They provide no moral guidance. Every question your kids may ask about sex gives you a golden opportunity to teach them the Christian view of sex and to guide their lives toward God's plan for their health and happiness.

Ten Messages Your Teenagers Should Know

The Bible says: **Be well-balanced — temperate, sober-minded; be vigilant and cautious at all times, for that enemy of yours, the devil, roams around like a lion roaring [in fierce hunger], seeking someone to seize upon and devour. Withstand him;...** (1 Peter 5:8,9 AMP).

Mark it down in your book: Satan is going to tempt your children with sexual sin. One of the best ways we know to resist him is with the truth.

Here are ten practical messages that will help your children when temptation comes. Teach them to your children so they won't be deceived by the devil and so they will be better prepared to resist him:

1. When someone says, "If you really love me, you'll have sex with me," it's always "a line" — an attempt to deceive you.

2. Girls get pregnant because they have sexual intercourse.

3. Girls can get pregnant the very first time they have sexual intercourse.

4. Sex is never a test or proof of love.

5. Sex is never a test or proof of masculinity or femininity. It doesn't make you any smarter, stronger, desirable or more mature.

110

6. "No" is a perfectly good oral contraceptive.

7. The vast majority of teenage girls who give birth are abandoned by the father of the child.[5]

8. Girls who feel they don't amount to anything unless some boy loves them should realize that self-worth never comes from someone else.

9. People who feel good about themselves generally will be more responsible in their sexual behavior. They don't have to prove anything.

10. Love and caring — not sex — is the most important thing in a boy/girl relationship. (Many surveys and studies among young people, as well as married couples, have proven this to be true.)

The Physical Consequences Can Be Fatal

Besides the moral consequences, you should also teach your children about the physical consequences of sex outside of marriage.

The greatest risk of premarital sex today is the virus known as AIDS, and there is no way of knowing who carries it and who doesn't. Age, sex, race, social position — nothing tells us who is infected and who isn't, and thousands of those already infected don't even know they have the disease.

Having premarital sex these days is like playing Russian roulette. Your son or daughter can never be sure if this time will be the fatal one. So why should they take a chance on something that could end their lives?

---

[5]Richard M. Lerner, Ann C. Peterson, and Jeanne Brooks-Gunn, *Encyclopedia of Adolescence*, 2 vols. (New York: Garland Publishing, 1991), 2:804.

Sexually Transmitted Diseases (STDs)[6]

Along with AIDS, there are other sexually transmitted diseases (STDs) that can cause things like sterility, blindness and even death. Formerly, there were only five diseases that were considered to be passed on by sexual contact. They were referred to as venereal diseases. Beginning in the 1960s, it was discovered that other diseases were also sexually transmitted. The term, STD, is used now, rather than venereal diseases, because it indicates a more comprehensive list of diseases that could be transmitted sexually.

STDs are a problem found among people of all ages and in all walks of life. However, more than half of the reported cases affect teenagers and young adults between the ages of 20 and 24. An estimated 1 out of 10 Americans contract some form of sexually transmitted disease each year.

Several factors seem to be contributing to the increase in STDs: 1) engaging in sex at an earlier age 2) engaging in sex with more than one partner 3) increasing the use of the pill and decreasing the use of condoms which helped reduce the risk.

STDs affect your sexual and reproductive organs and do not disappear even though the symptoms may go away on their own. If left untreated, both the carrier and the person he or she has had sexual contact with will also be affected.

The following is a list of some of the STDs along with their symptoms, how they are contracted and their effects:

---

[6]Based on *Collier's Encyclopedia*, s.v. "venereal disease," 1987.

AIDS (Acquired Immune Deficiency Syndrome)[7]

Symptoms: The most common early symptoms of the human immune deficiency virus (HIV) include fever, weight loss, enlarged lymph nodes, skin eruptions and shortness of breath. As the disease progresses, there may be drastic wasting, nausea, diarrhea, a rare type of pneumonia, neurological and visual impairment, and mental disturbances.

How you can get AIDS: Contact with infected body fluids or blood. Sexual contact or the use of a contaminated intraveneous needle, which can often be found among drug users, are the most common ways people contract AIDS. The infant of a mother infected with HIV may also be afflicted with the disease. Some people have contracted AIDS by receiving transfusions of HIV-tainted blood. However, a test has been developed that has enabled blood banks to screen their supplies of blood. Since small amounts of the AIDS virus are sometimes found in saliva, health experts advise against deep, prolonged kissing with someone who may be infected with the AIDS virus.

Most people who are infected with the AIDS virus look and feel fine. The only way to tell if you have the AIDS virus is by having a blood test. The test looks for changes in your blood caused by the presence of the virus. If you test positive, it means you have been infected. You can have the virus without developing the disease, or without even appearing ill. And you can transmit the virus to others. Once infected, you will remain infected for life.

Teenagers are encouraged to say "no" to sex and illegal drugs. Avoiding both drugs and sex is the best and safest

---

[7]Based on U.S. Public Health Service Centers for Disease Control and Prevention, Atlanta, *What You Should Know About AIDS*, (Washington, D.C.: GPO, 1989), pp. 3-6 and *Collier's Encylopedia*, s.v. "Acquired Immune Deficiency Syndrome (AIDS)."

way to eliminate the risk. Married couples should be mutually faithful. The risk of becoming infected with AIDS increases dramatically when anyone has more than one sexual partner. Risk is reduced by the use of condoms. Experts agree that sexual abstinance among those who are single or may be at risk is the best preventative measure against becoming infected with HIV.

Effects: Since no cure has been discovered for AIDS, it usually leads to death from multiple infections in a few months to three years from the time of onset.

Genital Chlamydia[8]

Symptoms: *Women*: White or yellow discharge, low back pain, painful menstruation, burning or pain while urinating, urinary frequency and urgency, spotting or bleeding. *Men*: White discharge, burning or pain while urinating.

How you can get chlamydia: By any type of sexual contact with a person who is infected with chlamydia. A baby can also get chlamydia when passing through the birth canal.

Effects: *Women*: Inflamation of the cervix, upper genital tract or pelvic area. *Men*: Inflamation of the urethra, rectum, epididymis or prostrate gland. If not treated, this disease can damage the reproductive organs, causing sterility in either the man or the woman.

Genital Herpes[9]

Symptoms: Can show up 3 - 7 days after sexual contact. Some people have no symptoms. Others experience raised

---

[8]Based on Stephen A. Schroeder et al., *Current Medical Diagnosis and Treatment 1989* (Norwalk, Connecticut: Appleton and Lange, 1989), p. 453, 923-924.

[9]Based on *Collier's Encyclopedia*, s.v. "venereal disease."

sores or fluid-filled blisters in the genital area which eventually disappear or burst to form shallow, painful sores that scab and heal. Blisters last 14 - 18 days then go away. A tingling, burning or itching sensation often occurs just before the sores reappear.

How you can get herpes: By any type of sexual contact with someone who has herpes. A baby can get a severe form of herpes if delivered through the birth canal. *Effects*: Genital herpes predisposes women to cervical cancer.

Gonorrhea (clap, drip, GC)[10]

Symptoms: Many women and some men have no symptoms; however, if symptoms do occur, it is usually within 2 - 10 days after sexual contact. *Women*: Discharge and pain or burning upon urination. *Men*: Thin milky-white or thick greenish-yellow discharge and an itching or burning sensation while urinating are the most common symptoms. Occasionally, blood streaks are present. In time, the symptoms will disappear, but the person is still infected.

How you can get gonorrhea: In practically all cases, gonorrhea is transmitted by direct contact, usually by sexual intercourse with someone who has gonorrhea. However, a mother, infected with gonorrhea, can give it to her baby during childbirth.

Effects: Gonorrhea can lead to a more serious disease which may cause sterility. If it gets into the bloodstream, arthritis, infection of the brain, blindness or even heart disease may occur.

NGU (nongonococcal or nonspecific urethritis, NSU)[11]

Symptoms: Often appear 1 - 3 weeks after exposure. Frequently women have no symptoms. *Women*: Burning

---

[10]Based on *Collier's Encyclopedia*, s.v. "venereal disease."

[11]Based on *Academic American Encyclopedia*, s.v. "venereal disease," 1989, and *The Encyclopedia Americana*, s.v. "venereal disease," 1991.

during urination and a mild vaginal discharge. *Men:* Mild mucous discharge accompanied by feelings of discomfort while urinating.

How you can get NGU: One of the ways NGU can be contracted is through sexual contact, but this is *not* the only way. At present, all the causes of this disease are not fully understood; however, it is the most common complaint of men in STD clinics.

Effects: Women: Sterility, miscarriages, tubal pregnancies and eye infections in newborn babies. *Men:* sterility.

Syphilis[12]

Symptoms: Syphilis occurs in several stages, which are very much the same in both men and women.

First Stage: These symptoms appear 10 - 90 days after exposure. A small painless chancre, pimple or open ulcer usually develops in the gential area but may appear on the breast, lip, tongue, face or finger. Discharges from the chancre are very contagious. *Second Stage:* These symptoms usually appear 6 - 10 weeks after exposure. By this time, the chancre has disappeared, even without treatment, and a skin rash may appear anywhere on the body or ulcers develop in the mouth or around the gential area. These symptoms eventually disappear. *Third Stage:* The symptoms may remain latent for 1 - 20 years. In this last phase, the individual may develop large sores that invade the bone or liver and may experience damage to the heart, blood vessels, brain and spinal cord.

How you can get syphilis: By having sexual intercourse, kissing or touching the rash or open sore of a person with syphilis. A mother can give syphilis to her baby even before birth.

---

[12]Based on *Collier's Encyclopedia,* s.v. "venereal disease."

Effects: Syphilis, once it reaches the third stage, can cause heart disease, insanity, blindness, paralysis and death.

Vaginitis (bacterial vaginosis, trich, yeast)[13]

Symptoms: Vaginal irritation and a cheesy white discharge with an offensive odor.

How you can get vaginitis: The transmission of vaginitis is not understood very well, even though it is the most common complaint of women in STD clinics. It may be associated with pregnancy, antibiotics, diabetes, birth control pills or, in some cases, sexual contact. (Note that sexual activity is not always the cause of vaginitis; if your child contracts vaginitis, it does not mean the child has been sexually active.) Male sex partners may also be carriers of vaginitis and must be treated, even though they have no apparent symptoms.

Effects: Without treatment, uncomfortable symptoms will continue.

Venereal Warts[14]

Symptoms: May appear up to 3 months after sexual contact. Rough-surfaced bumps or warts in the genital area. They may be single but are usually multiple and do not itch.

How you can get genital warts: By any type of sexual contact with someone who has genital warts.

Effects: The warts may indicate a precancerous condition.

What To Do About STD Symptoms

When STD symptoms are present, testing and treatment of both sexual partners are required. The best prevention

---

[13]Based on *The Encyclopedia Americana International Edition*, s.v. "venereal disease."

[14]Based on *Academic American Encyclopedia*, s.v. "venereal disease."

measure against the pain, embarrassment and toll on your physical health in general is sexual abstinence. If married, the best prevention is mutual faithfulness to the marriage vows.

Sex the way God intended it to be is wonderful, but anything else will bring heartache and ruin. That's what God's Word says, and that's what our children have to know.

10
Protect Your Children From Abuse and Abduction

Child abuse is not a new problem. As long as man has been sinning, he has been taking advantage of the weak and helpless. The Bible has many stories of child abuse, and it records God's anger about it.

In Jeremiah 32, the Lord tells the prophet that He is about to hand the children of Israel over to the Babylonians because of their wickedness. He says:

> **For the children of Israel and the children of Judah have only done evil before me from their youth....**
>
> **And they built the high places of Baal, which are in the valley of the son of Hinnom, to cause their sons and their daughters to pass through the fire unto Molech; which I commanded them not, neither came it into my mind, that they should do this abomination, to cause Judah to sin.**

> **vv. 30,35**

Child sacrifice was — and is — so offensive to God that He says the thought of it had never even entered His mind.

Even in New Testament times, child abuse and immorality were practiced. When the apostle Paul wrote to the Ephesian church, he told them to **have no fellowship with the unfruitful works of darkness, but rather reprove them. For it is a shame even to speak of those things which are done of them** [the wicked] **in secret** (Eph. 5:11,12).

It is a shame that things like child abuse exist in our world today. It makes us ashamed as human beings that people are molesting, abusing and killing innocent children. But the sad fact is that these things are happening around us, and we have to prepare our children to deal with them.

So often in the past as kids were growing up, they may have overheard their parents and other adults talking quietly about cases of child abuse and molestation. But it wasn't discussed openly back then. For the most part, people weren't willing to admit that the problem of child abuse really existed except in isolated incidents. And when child abuse was discovered, even fewer people were willing to get involved.

Today the problem is finally out in the open. There are always newspaper stories or reports on TV about how someone somewhere abused a child. The bad news is that for every case of abuse reported, there are many, many others kept quiet. In fact, child abuse could be called the most under-reported crime in the United States.

Violence in the Home

How sad it is when we read about a father who beat his infant son to death because the child wouldn't quit crying. When rushed to the hospital, the baby was pronounced dead as a result of repeated blows to his head. Even if the baby had lived, he would have been brain damaged.

There was also the story of a mother and her boyfriend who handcuffed her adolescent son to a fencepost at their home. They left him there for several days without food or water with temperatures going over 100 degrees. That was his punishment for running away from home!

We have all heard horror stories about kids who were abused in homes, churches, schools — even in preschools. A number of years ago, one case involved several preschool teachers who were charged with 200 counts of horrible sex crimes against those little kids.

Finally in the 1960s every state passed laws to cover the reporting of child abuse. Then in the early 1970s, the federal government created the National Center on Child Abuse and Neglect in an effort to fight the problem.

Thank God the problem is being brought out into the open, and more is being done to overcome this tragedy. But we still have a long way to go.

That well-known case involving abuse in the preschool has played a major role in current child-abuse legislation. In that state today, schools and preschools are teaching children that they have the right to be free from abuse and how to defend themselves against it.

What Is Child Abuse?

One of the biggest problems with child abuse is deciding what it really is. What some people consider normal treatment of children, others feel is abuse. The confusion and fear has become so great among many school boards and state legislatures that they have outlawed any kind of corporal punishment in their schools for fear of being accused of abuse.

So what is abuse?

Abuse is any physical, verbal, sexual or emotional treatment of a child that is motivated by the parent's own anger and hostility. That parent lacks the desire to positively change his child's behavior or to do what is best for him.

In other words, abuse happens when an adult does what he considers is good for himself even though it hurts the child. He reacts in his own selfish interest rather than in the child's best interest. Haven't we all been embarrassed when we saw a parent humiliate a child in public or strike him in anger for something as simple as spilling food or knocking over a glass of water?

Each state has written its own legislation on child abuse. In Oklahoma, where we live, according to Title 21, Section 845 of the Oklahoma Statutes, "'Abuse and neglect,' means harm or threatened harm to a child's health or welfare...." Harm or threatened harm to a child's health or welfare can occur through: nonaccidental physical or mental injury, sexual abuse or neglect. In a publication produced by the Oklahoma State Department of Health Child Guidance Service[1] each of these means is further defined:

> *Nonaccidental physical injury* may include beatings, shaking, burns, human bites, strangulation or immersion in scalding water with resulting bruises and welts, broken bones, scars or internal injuries.

> *Psychological maltreatment* is generally recognized as either psychological neglect or psychological abuse. Psychological neglect is the consistent failure of a parent or caretaker to provide a child with appropriate support, attention and affection. Psychological abuse is a chronic pattern of behaviors such as belittling, humiliating and ridiculing a child.

> *Sexual abuse* is the exploitation of a child or adolescent for the sexual gratification of another person. It includes behaviors such as intercourse, sodomy, oral-genital stimulation, verbal stimulation, exhibitionism, voyeurism, fondling and involving a child in prostitution or the production of pornography.

> *Neglect* is the failure to provide a child with basic needs such as food, clothing, shelter, medical care, educational opportunity, protection and supervision.

---

[1]Based on *For Kids' Sake: A Child Abuse Prevention and Reporting Kit*, rev. ed. (Capitol Bancnote Printing, 1992), pp. 4,8,10,12,14.

The publication also states:

• If you have reason to believe that a child under 18 has been abused, then you are mandated by law to report the suspected abuse. A person making a report in good faith is immune from both civil and criminal liability. Failure to do so is considered a crime. If additional incidents of abuse occur after the initial report has been made, make another request for investigation.

The sad part is that children who were abused often grow up to abuse their own children. They treat their kids the way their parents treated them because they don't know anything else. They have never seen good parenting. So without outside help, the abuse will continue generation after generation.

Why Child Abuse Happens

All of us parents experience frustration and anger when our children defy us, when they talk back or when they don't do what we tell them to do. Our patience runs out, we wear down and we eventually reach the end of our rope.

We have all had days when we feel misunderstood, overworked and unappreciated as a parent. That's normal. It's also normal and common in our lives to have days when nothing goes right and the kids get on our nerves. When we come home from work exhausted, we are too tired to deal with them and their problems.

This is a real problem for single parents who have to deal with everything by themselves. There's no one to step in and take over when they come home from work after a hard day. There's no one to help with the bills, no one to take the car to the shop when it breaks down, no one to stay home when the kids get sick. In situations like this, it's easy to become frustrated and angry.

Most adults are able to handle life's frustrations and upsets pretty well. They are able to cope when the car breaks down, or when someone fails to keep his word, or when they receive that second notice in the mail about an overdue bill.

Others, however, can't seem to cope with even the smallest crisis. An argument, or tension at work, or a stubborn child can cause abuse. These parents don't seem to be able to handle life's problems. Most of them love their kids, but when their despair and frustration is more than they can handle, their pattern is to take it out on those closest to them — the little ones who can't fight back.

So many things can contribute to child abuse by parents, such as their own abusive childhood, a feeling of stress, poverty, discrimination, lack of parenting skills, inadequate child care, psychological immaturity, mental illness, alcoholism and drug addiction. A growing cause of child abuse is the increasing number of combined families — when divorced parents remarry bringing together children from previous marriages, and then add to them new children from their union.

Whatever the cause, child abuse is a hard fact of life. We must all face it and work to find answers.

"What Can I Do?"

If you consider yourself to be an abusive parent, remember, there is help for both you and your children.

1. Go to God, Confess Your Sin, and Ask for His Forgiveness

There is no sin too big or too terrible for God to forgive. First John 1:9 says, **If we confess our sins, he is faithful and just to forgive us our sins, and to cleanse us from all unrighteousness.**

Ask Him to help you overcome your abuse and then help you become the kind of parent He wants you to be.

2. Go to Someone You Trust for Help — Your Pastor or a Trained Christian Counselor

Through prayer and counseling, you can change. You can learn how to cope with your problems in a positive way so you can be a loving parent. You can learn to discipline your children in love, without anger or fear.

3. Get Help for Your Children

Even though you may never abuse your children again, they still need help for the hurts that were inflicted upon them in the past. They need the same healing — mental, physical and spiritual — that you need.

So often when kids are abused they think it is because they are bad and they somehow deserve to be abused. They don't like who they are. They feel worthless and hopeless. Without outside help, they grow up with these feelings and often become abusive parents themselves.

Pray for your children. Do whatever you can to help them toward healing and wholeness. If necessary, confess your wrongdoing to them and ask for their forgiveness. Just letting them know that you — and not them — are at fault can help tremendously towards their recovery.

Christians Can Be Abusive Parents

Some people have a hard time believing that Christians abuse their kids. They think, "How can that be?"

It would be wonderful if becoming a Christian would automatically make us perfect, but that isn't how it works. When we are born again, God destroys our old sinful nature and puts His nature within us. The apostle Peter says we are partakers of the divine nature of God. (2 Peter 1:4.) That's power! Our mortal flesh is touched with immortality, and a change begins to take place.

Although God does heal and deliver instantly, the change of conforming to the image of Christ is gradual. It's a day-to-day process that continues until we go to be with the Lord. If you bring a totally undisciplined past into your new relationship with Jesus, it doesn't just disappear overnight because you became a Christian. You have a new God-like nature, but you have to grow and mature in Him, learning how to handle your life in a way that will be pleasing to Him.

That's why discipleship is so important. There should be a time for daily prayer, Bible study and, when necessary, spiritual counseling. You have to bring your weaknesses and inadequacies to Jesus Christ, and have a teachable spirit and a willing, obedient heart. Then God's power will begin to work in you, enabling you to overcome the bad habits and inadequacies left over from your past life. God's Holy Spirit will give you the power to change.

God also uses other people to help us change. While prayer and Bible study are essential to help us grow, we also need the help of people around us to reach wholeness. Abusive parents especially need practical help to learn how to cope and be the kind of parent they desire to be. They need trained Christian counselors to help them overcome the devastation of child abuse.

Child abuse is such a far-reaching problem that we can't afford to spiritualize it, making it appear that one trip to the altar will totally solve the problem in every person who abused his children. Deep-rooted problems like this need some serious things to bring about the solution: prayer, persistence, the Word of God, education, support, counseling. And reality tells us that to achieve wholeness, we have to take advantage of every means of practical help that is available.

What About Molestation and Abduction?

When we were growing up, a parent's role as protector for the most part meant protecting his child from injury, usually caused by the child's own irresponsibility. Today parents have a much tougher job. They not only have to protect their kids from normal childhood injury, but they have to protect them from injury from other adults as well as from possible abduction.

What's the best way to protect your children from molestation and abduction? First of all, you should know about the dangers surrounding them in today's world and then educate them about these dangers.

Many Christian parents are naive as to the subtle and devious ways child molesters and abductors think and work. They try to ignore the problem in hopes that it will never happen to them.

We encourage you to learn about these two subjects. Educate yourself about how children can be deceived and lured by an abductor for the purposes of sexual molestation, abduction and even murder. Jesus told His followers, **...be ye therefore wise as serpents, and harmless as doves** (Matt. 10:16).

The second important thing to do is trust God. We firmly believe that we must commit ourselves and our families to God and live according to His Word. When we do, He will put His supernatural covering of protection around us to keep us from the evil one. Psalm 34:7,8 says, **The angel of the Lord encampeth round about them that fear him, and delivereth them. O taste and see that the Lord is good: blessed is the man that trusteth in him.**

We need to balance the confidence we have in God's protection with the wisdom He gives us for the practical everyday things. We don't have to be afraid because we trust in Him, but we also should be alert as parents. We should learn of the possible dangers and do all we can to keep our children from them.

What You Should Do If You Suspect Child Abuse

If you have reason to suspect that your child is being or has been abused, act immediately. Call the police department or contact your local child welfare department for guidance in handling the problem.

As soon as possible, take your child to a physician to see if any physical harm has occurred.

Above all, reassure your child that he didn't do anything wrong and that you love him. The important thing is for you to get help at once. The life and well-being of your child is the most important consideration of all!

You Can Help an Abused Child

What should you do if you know a child is being abused? Because every situation is different, there isn't one simple answer. But one thing we can say is this: *do something!* Don't ignore the problem and pretend it will go away. If you do, we believe God will hold you accountable because you could have helped but didn't.

We suggest that you go to your pastor or a Christian counselor when you have information about an abused child. Ask for their help. Counselors usually know the laws regarding child abuse and can give you some direction.

Also pray for the child and his parents. Most abusive parents love their children, but they need help learning how to cope with their personal problems. The abused child especially needs prayer. When his parents are not Christians, the child has a distorted view of Who God is, and he may reject God because of his parents' actions.

It's equally important that we as Christians show forgiveness to abusive Christian parents who have asked God's forgiveness and are working to change. They must also be taught how to forgive themselves for their actions. They have to learn how to trust one another and God again. And they have to deal with each other in love and tenderness.

We believe it's the Church's role to teach Christians how to deal with these frustrations in positive ways. We need to learn that anger is not bad when expressed in the right way. It becomes bad when we lash out at our kids and express it in harsh ways.

God's Word says, *When angry, do not sin* (Eph. 4:26 AMP). It doesn't say, "Don't be angry." It is saying it's okay to be angry in the right way. It's impossible for us to never be angry. It's also not scriptural. There are times when we need to be angry. In the Old Testament God got angry when people rebelled against Him and did all manner of evil in His sight. When we get angry, we need to express our anger in the right way — not by abusing someone else.

If after reading this you feel you are abusing your children, or if you know someone who is, we urge you to get help immediately. Don't wait. Innocent lives are in the balance. There is help available. So get help now, before it's too late!

Five Ways Parents Set
Their Children Up for Exploitation[2]

"Good" kids make ideal victims because they are taught:

---

[2]Based on an article by Joanne Ross Feldmeth, "Child Molestation: Why Good Kids Make Good Victims," *Focus on the Family*, November 1984.

1. "Respect Your Elders"

If an adult tells you to do something, do it. While children must be taught obedience and respect for authority, they must also understand that they have the right — like Daniel, Esther and the apostle Peter — to stand against authority that is being misused.

Tell your child that if an adult — even a teacher, preacher, doctor, relative or anybody — wants to touch him in a way that makes him feel uncomfortable because of how or where he is touched, or wants him to do something that he feels is wrong, your child has a right to say NO!

2. "Don't Be a Tattletale!"

A molester will often threaten a child if he or she tells what has happened. Tell your child that if an adult tells him *not* to tell anyone else what he is doing, then he *should* tell because it is probably wrong. Teach your child how to call the police and how to reach you at home or work.

3. "Children Should Be Seen and Not Heard"

Children often complain that parents don't listen to them. It is important that you listen to your children. Take your child's feelings seriously. Be on the lookout for phrases that might mean trouble. If your son complains that a relative or family friend makes him feel "yukky," try to find out why. If your daughter tells you she is being molested, believe it! Children rarely lie about sexual abuse.

4. "Nice People Don't Talk About Things Like That"

A child who is never allowed to talk about his sexual feelings with Mom or Dad will, in all likelihood, be unable to tell them if he is being molested.

5. "You're Too Big To Cuddle"

Some parents are afraid that if they cuddle their children, especially teenagers, it might lead to incest or accusations of incest. Child psychologists tell us that warmth and affection don't cause sexual problems but may in reality prevent them.

As children begin to grow up, some parents withdraw physically. They don't show their child outward signs of affection as they did when the child was smaller. And some children interpret this as rejection. Professionals point out that a lack of outward warmth from a parent makes a child more vulnerable to molesters.

Molesters develop a special sensitivity to children and can spot symptoms of vulnerability. They can analyze dress and playground behavior. They look for a withdrawn child who is apparently depressed — a loner — a child who plays with younger children rather than with peers.

How You Can Protect
Your Children From Abduction[3]

1. Watch your children closely at all times. Don't leave them alone in the car while you are shopping or running errands, alone in the yard or unattended in a store or other public place. Know where your child is.

2. Understand that placing your child's name on his or her schoolbooks and belongings puts a potential abductor on a first-name basis with your child.

3. Have your child fingerprinted and keep the prints at home in a safe place, along with a recent picture of your child. If your child ever turns up missing, this may be your best bet to locate your child.

4. Encourage your neighbors to participate in a neighborhood self-help program. For example, by establishing a safe home where kids can go for help.

---

[3]Mitch McConnell, Chairman of the Kentucky Task Force on Exploited and Missing Children. Used by permission.

5. Encourage your school principal to immediately notify parents whose children do not report to school. If the principal claims that this is too much of a burden, offer to form a volunteer group to help notify parents.

Remember, the battle to protect our children begins at home — in the family, in the neighborhood, in the school and in the church.

Signals of Sexual Abuse[4]

Extensive studies tell us that one in every five victims of sexual abuse is a child under seven years old. Therefore, parents must learn the signs children give that signal abuse. The following signs could be giving off such a message:

- Appears withdrawn or becomes excessively active
- Has a poor relationship with other children of the same age
- Regresses into baby-like behavior
- Seems unusually fearful, especially of adults
- Acts more like an adult than a child
- Begins to do poorly in school and there is a sudden change in his or her grades
- Has a sudden change in appetite
- Becomes sexually promiscuous or provocative in the way he or she dresses or acts
- Engages in compulsive masturbation
- Sexually abuses a brother, sister, friend or younger child
- Runs away from home

---

[4]American Medical Association, *Diagnostic and Treatment Guidelines on Child Sexual Abuse* (Chicago: American Medical Association), p. 8.

Don't close your eyes if you see any of these signals from your child or another child.

Support Groups for Abusive Parents

There are many support groups available for abusive parents. Parents Anonymous chapters throughout the country offer non-judgmental help. Their toll-free number is 1-800-421-0353.

Another organization is Stop Child Abuse Now, known as SCAN. You can get their telephone number as well as numbers of any local agencies available in your town or city in the yellow pages of your telephone directory under "Child Abuse." The United Way has Family/Children Service agencies in major cities which can also provide you with informative literature and counseling.

11

What You Should Know About Drug and Tobacco Abuse

One of the biggest threats facing families today is drug abuse. By drugs, we mean all the junk that people take in by swallowing, smoking, sniffing, injecting, inhaling, chewing, dipping and drinking. These various types of drugs are harmful to their bodies, minds and spirits.

The apostle Paul said in 1 Corinthians 6:19,20:

> **What? know ye not that your body is the temple of the Holy Ghost which is in you, which ye have of God, and ye are not your own?**
>
> **For ye are bought with a price: therefore glorify God in your body, and in your spirit, which are God's.**

God never intended for our bodies to be sewers, but that's what drugs will turn you into when you abuse them. There are so many drugs going around today that no one can keep up with them. Every few months some new drug craze sweeps the country. As a result, there are broken minds, bodies and spirits left behind.

Drugs are stealing from the lives of our young people, and it's time we did something about it. No family is safe from it.

So what can you do? Train your children in the ways we have already discussed to keep them from experimenting with drugs.

1. Inform your children about drugs so that they will not be caught by surprise and give in to peer pressure. Inform them so that they will be prepared to "just say no."

2. Build up your children's self-esteem. Teach them who they are in Christ; tell them they are winners!

3. Teach your children to respect godly authority; at an early age, instill in them a reverence for God so that they will not want to rebel.

4. Be consistent with the rules. They will know that there will be consequences for disobeying your rule to not use drugs.

5. Keep your children involved in church and church activities to help them continue to choose friends who are good for them. Stay acquainted with their friends.

6. Spend time together. Keep the lines of communication open so that your children know they can go to you and talk about anything.

7. Encourage them to have a positive effect on those around them by standing up for what they believe.

8. Set a good example yourself. Do you unconsciously project an attitude that substances are to be used to help you feel better, even if they hurt you physically, by drinking or smoking?

9. Know how and where to get help, and if you need it, get it.

10. Throw your care over on the Lord. As hard as it is to go through this if your child is using drugs, remember that God can stop and turn to the good that which the devil meant for evil.

11. Keep showing your child that you love him unconditionally, and keep praying for him.

Become Familiar With Some Common Signs of Drug Abuse[1]

Dr. Dale Doty, founder of Christian Family Institute in Tulsa, Oklahoma, is a licensed Marriage and Family Therapist, who works with drug abusers and their families to bring about positive change in their lives. In a recent interview, he cited the following common signs of drug abuse.

Physical Changes

- Pupils of the eyes are inappropriate in size and are not responsive to changes in lighting.

- Sleep patterns may become irregular as drug users may often be up during the night hours then have difficulty getting up in the morning, causing them to be tardy or to accumulate a number of unexplained absenses.

- Their appetite either increases or, more often than not, decreases as they begin to miss meals or refuse to eat.

- Speech often becomes slurred, and they may forget what they were saying in the middle of a conversation.

- Although many drugs today are taken orally, some are taken intravenously. In these instances, needle marks may appear, usually on the arms.

- A change in the way a person dresses may indicate that they are now identifying with a different group of friends.

---

[1]From an interview with Dale Doty, Director of Training, Christian Family Institute, March 1993. Used by permission.

Social Changes

- Their familiar peer network changes. Old friends begin to drop off as new friends gain more of their attention.

- They display anti-social behavior around the family and tend to withdraw from their activities.

- They become more and more secretive. When questioned about what they have been doing and where they have been, their response is usually defensive.

- Manipulative and controlling type behaviors increase. The most common type of manipulative behaviors are lying and overt deception. When these happen, inconsistencies in word and deed will become more noticable.

- Increased amounts of time will not be able to be accounted for.

- They may be using the phone at unusual times, calling people late at night or early in the morning.

- They may also begin staying out later and later at night without any particular reason.

- They or a friend of theirs may even be carrying a pager around for no apparent reason.

Emotional Changes

- Their anger or resentment increases especially when questions are asked.

- They show disrespect for authority.

- They become increasingly more moody and irritable.

- Their behavior may be extremely stimulated to the point that they can't sit still or are unusually passive and inactive.

- They may laugh inappropriately and appear to be giddy.

- They typically display a basic mistrust of people and may seem to be excessively paranoid or fearful.

Scholastic Changes

- Their grades at school will usually drop drastically because they have more difficulty concentrating.

- They may be getting into trouble more often than usual while at school.

- Their memory may be slightly impaired. As a result, they will frequently forget to do things that they had been responsible for previously.

Financial Changes

- They may be carrying around unusually large amounts of money.

- Occasionally, various amounts of money may even be missing.

Spiritual Changes

- They may refuse to go to church and become increasingly hostile towards God and the people involved within church.

- They may even go to the other extreme and be ambivalent or act disinterested in church.

- Eventually, their moral values may be replaced with more promiscuous ones.

Dr. Doty cautions that all of these signs can and may be related to causes other than drug abuse. Therefore, you should not presume that drug abuse is the reason for a particular behavior without investigating further. If a parent falsely accuses a child of drug abuse, alienation may result.

However, Dr. Doty also states, "If a number of these signs persist on a regular basis, you as a parent do have the responsibility of finding out why they exist, and I would strongly recommend that a physician or counselor become involved in the process. A blood or urine test the day after the suspected use of a drug would help provide conclusive evidence of the problem so that proper treatment could begin."

Even though it is difficult to recognize if a person is abusing drugs, don't be naive in thinking that it couldn't happen to your child. Be alert. Recognize the signs. Then take the necessary steps to receive help so you and your family can continue to walk in the victory that God has planned for you.

12
Christian School or Public School? How To Choose

Christian parents often wonder about the value of Christian education. They say, "Does it really make any difference whether we send our kids to a Christian school or a public school?" It's not an easy question to answer.

During the time our parents were growing up, public schools taught the same basic principles that were taught at home. Children could be taught the Lord's Prayer in grade school as well as the Pledge of Allegiance to the flag. The three "Rs" of education — *readin', 'riting and 'rithmatic* — were the priority. Children learned that it was wrong to lie, steal and hurt other people. And they were taught to honor their parents, their teachers, their country — and God.

Today, things are very different. Teachers aren't allowed to talk to their students about morals, the Bible or God. And, for the most part, they aren't even allowed to discipline the kids. The idea of humanism seems strong in public education, while anything hinting at Christianity has been declared illegal by the Supreme Court and erased from our public education system. Things are so bad in some schools that students are graduating without knowing how to read or write enough to survive in our world today.

The Issue of Prayer in the Schools

For many people, the controversy centers on the issue of prayer in public schools, but this isn't really the main issue. While getting prayer back in school might be a good first step toward getting God back in our public education system, we might also be opening the proverbial Pandora's Box. A multitude of new issues and problems would arise like these: Who will lead the prayer? What are his or her personal beliefs about God? Who are they praying to? What is the meaning of the prayer? How is God being portrayed?

There are so many issues involved in the prayer controversy that we could be getting sidetracked from other more important issues. We can't determine the quality of education our children are receiving based only on whether or not they are allowed to pray in their classrooms. Even if a child was allowed to pray in school, he might still be receiving a secular, humanistic education.

When it comes to choosing the best type of education for our kids, it isn't simply a matter of Christian education versus secular education. There are many other factors to consider, including:

- How much time and energy are you as a parent willing to give to your child's education?

- What kind of Christian schools are available in your area?

- How strongly does your area's public schools adhere to the humanist philosophy?

- What kind of financial commitment are you willing and able to make?

What Is Humanism?

Perhaps the greatest danger in public schools today is the philosophy of humanism. When you mention the word *humanism* to many Christians, they say, "Oh yes, that's bad." But they may not really understand what humanism is or why it's so dangerous and wrong.

Putting it simply, the humanist philosophy does away with God and puts man in God's place. Humanism says that the individual — not God — is the most important thing in the universe.

The humanist thinking goes something like this: "I decide right and wrong based upon what's right and wrong for me at any particular moment. I decide what I should do with my life and how I should live. And I alone am responsible for saving myself and making myself better."

The result of this way of thinking is the idea that there are no universal moral laws in life. Each person does whatever he feels is right for him at that particular moment. Nothing is really wrong for a humanist if that is what he wants and needs.

Some humanists feel that children — and not their parents — should make their own moral decisions. To them, no one person can tell another what is right or wrong for him, because what is wrong for him may be right for someone else.

This way of thinking completely undermines authority — yours, God's, the government's, the school's. How can we make laws if each person is a law unto himself? It destroys every moral law in the Bible and eliminates compassion and self-sacrifice for others. To the humanist, no one is more important than "me."

For humanists there are no such things as sin, guilt and repentance. To them, people aren't really bad or sinful; they are simply misguided, misinformed or confused, and they need to be taught a more acceptable, positive way of living. To them, education is the answer to all our problems. It's the religion of self-improvement. To them, people do bad things because they don't realize they have better alternatives.

Humanists believe that man — and man alone — can make himself better. They say that with education and hard work we can make ourselves and our world perfect if we all try. They say we don't need some god to save us and forgive us; we can save ourselves.

Humanists don't believe Jesus is God. To them, He was only a good man Who was brutally killed and misunderstood by His followers. In their thinking, He was no more a god than we are.

You may ask, "Then where did we come from?"

The humanists will tell you that man evolved, just as the universe and all animal and plant life evolved. In their mind, man is a product of natural forces — not supernatural. They see our belief in God and Satan as simply a myth that our ancestors created as a way to help us understand our world and deal with the processes of life and death.

To the humanist, there is no life after death because man is only an animal without a soul. The only life we have is the life here and now, so we need to enjoy ourselves and make the best of it.

Do you see why this philosophy is dangerous? It's the same philosophy Satan used on Eve in the Garden of Eden. **But the serpent said to the woman, For God knows that in the day you eat of it** [the fruit] **your eyes will be opened, and you will be as God, knowing the difference between good and evil, and blessing and calamity** (Gen. 3:4,5 AMP).

Since the beginning of time, man has been trying to become a god. Humanism isn't a new philosophy — it's the oldest philosophy there is! We are still trying to set ourselves up as God, and humanism is just the fancy new name we are calling our efforts.

The "Magic Circle"

There has been a group going around to public and private schools promoting a program which they claim reinforces children's self-esteem. But actually the program promotes the humanistic doctrine.

For example, part of the program is a game called the "Magic Circle." In it, an instructor asks the children, "Does anybody believe Jesus Christ is the Son of God?" If a child raises his hand, the instructor points at him and asks, "Do you really believe Jesus is the Son of God?" If the child again says yes, the instructor draws a "magic circle." He tells the kids that the circle has to do with accepting who they are. Then he lets all of them — except that one child — stand inside the circle. That child has to stay outside, and he can't take part in any of the activities the other kids are doing.

From time to time throughout the day, the teacher again asks that child, "Do you really believe Jesus is the Son of God?" As long as the child says yes, he has to stand outside that "magic circle." Finally, the child catches on and answers the teacher by saying, "No, I don't believe Jesus is the Son of God." At that point, the teacher welcomes him into the magic circle.

We heard how a representative of that group called one teacher at a Christian school and offered to "help" her children by coming in with their program. As soon as he told her about the program, she knew what it was. When she asked him for a pamphlet or brochure telling about the program or about the group's research, he never called her back. He knew they had been found out!

Humanism in the Schools

You may ask, "If the philosophy of humanism is so bad, then why have our schools promoted it?"

Schools are promoting humanism largely by default. We expect them to teach moral behavior, right thinking and self-improvement, but they aren't allowed to talk about the basis for all those things, which is God. So the schools use humanism as their basis because they have nothing else.

Please understand, not all teachers are humanists or bad. The majority are good people who mean well, but they are strictly limited in what they can teach. They are required to use approved curriculum. They are told what they can and cannot say. They have to teach moral living without teaching God-given morality, and that always results in humanism. When God is eliminated, man is all that's left.

When we take God out of creation, we have evolution. When we take away man's soul, he becomes a mere animal. When we do away with eternity, we are left with only sensual living. And when we take God out of our morality, we are left with immorality.

The simplest examples of humanistic thinking to a parent could sound something like this:

- Why shouldn't our teenagers have sex before marriage if it feels good? After all, they are only following a natural urge.

- And what's so special about marriage anyway? It's just a legal contract.

- Why shouldn't kids cheat to get ahead in school? Isn't that what life is all about — getting ahead, being a success?

- Why shouldn't they party it up and enjoy some drugs? After all, you only live once, so you have to grab the gusto!

Of course, humanism hasn't worked in our schools or in our society, and it never will. No philosophy that leaves

God out or moves Him from His rightful place will ever succeed.

We have tried to keep the teenagers from indulging in premarital sex by simply educating them about the dangers involved. Teenagers today know more about sex and its consequences than any previous generation. Yet, the number of unwed pregnancies, abortions, venereal diseases, etc., have continued to grow.

We have tried to educate the young people about the dangers of drugs and drinking, but more and more teenagers are dying from accidents due to alcohol and drugs.

We have given children a moral system built on shifting sand and a future without hope. Consequently, the number of suicides among teenagers continues to go up. And this has become the most materialistic generation in history.

The truth is, we can't save ourselves; we can't help ourselves. We were born in a world of sin with no righteousness of our own. Without God, we are without hope. But in Jesus Christ, we have hope. He gives us meaning. He is the Solid Rock that will never move. And He gives us life beyond the grave.

As a result of our children being exposed to humanism in public schools, there is a multitude of problems. First, humanism isn't true — it's a lie, and our kids will be learning a lie. Second, it conflicts with the moral teaching they are learning at home and at church. They can become confused about what the truth really is. Third, humanism undermines our authority as parents and creates doubts in our children's minds about our leadership.

Kids are so susceptible to outside influences. They can't discern the truth like we adults can. Because we teach them to respect authority, including their teachers, they believe what their teachers tell them. And they are with their teachers more than with us. That means what their teachers are telling them is having a profound influence on their lives. So we must be sure that their teachers are telling them the truth!

Other Problems in Public Schools

Of course, humanism is only one of the problems in public schools today. Other problems are drugs, gangs, race relations, physical assaults, etc. Students are being pressured to participate in things that aren't good for them, and they pick up values that conflict with the Christian values we are teaching them.

Many public schools have completely lost their focus on the basics of education. They are graduating students who can't read or write above the second- or third-grade level. And some schools seem to care more about their basketball and football records than they do about academics.

In our opinion, all of these are good reasons to put your children in a Christian school. Children can't learn when they are always facing serious problems like those found in public schools today: too many students in one room, poor facilities, some kids strung out on drugs, kids afraid of being assaulted by other kids. Children in school shouldn't have to spend their energy trying to survive.

Now, Christian schools aren't perfect, but we believe that, for the most part, they are more valuable than public schools. In so many ways, public schools have many problems that hinder education.

We feel that children can get a better education through private Christian schools and at the same time can escape most of the problems that are in city schools. Their education will also prepare them for every station of life, whether it be a blue-collar job, a career or a family.

Through Christian schools kids are helped to become people who open themselves up to the fruit of the Spirit and who are raised in the discipline of the Lord. They receive teaching and training from these schools that compliment the teaching and training they receive at home.

This is the kind of instruction that provides our students with a Christ-centered education which is second to none.

Choosing a Christian School

So, how do you choose a good Christian school? There are several things to consider.

1. Is It a Real Christian School?

Don't be fooled into thinking that just because a school calls itself "Christian" it really is. Find out what the school teaches and endorses. Does it teach truth that is Bible-based and Christ-centered? And is that truth mixed throughout every stage of learning? Ask for a statement of the school's beliefs. Talk to the teachers and administrators about the principles which their school endorses and upholds.

2. Does the School Have a Good Curriculum Base?

Observe its teachers and staff to see if they know what they are doing. Visit the classrooms and listen to what is being taught there. Ask around your community and find out what kind of reputation the school has in academic circles. Find out what kind of education its teachers are required to have.

3. Are the Classes Overcrowded or Small?

Most Christian schools provide the smaller classroom environment so there can be more of a one-on-one between the teacher and students. That allows better learning for the students, and students who need help get it more quickly.

4. Does the School Require Discipline, and If So, Are the Students Disciplined in Love?

Before a child can learn, he must know how to sit still in his seat and be cooperative and obedient. The only way this happens is by disciplining his self-will — by teaching him how to have a right relationship before God and by using biblical discipline.

Find out what is expected of the students and what kind of discipline the school uses, so you can get a clear picture of what the school requires. Is corporal punishment inflicted? If so, how much and when?

5. Do the Teachers Really Care About Their Students and Pray for Them As Well As Teach Them?

You need to look for a Christian school where the teachers believe in the power of prayer. In addition to the mental teaching of a child, there needs to be spiritual teaching. There should be a love between the teachers and students. The teachers should be praying for them and working to draw out their students' gifts and talents. Then the children's self-esteem will be strengthened, and they will want to accelerate.

6. How Much Does the School Cost, and Are the School Officials Willing to Work With You in Paying the Fee?

Many Christian schools are sponsored and supported by churches. They may have scholarships and other financial aids to help parents who want their kids in a Christian school. When you talk to the school officials, ask about financial aid.

Of course, it's going to cost you to enroll your children in a private Christian school. Good education is expensive. But the question is not: *How can I afford to send my children to a Christian school?* With the state of public education as it is today, the question may be: *How can I not afford to send my children to a Christian school?*

No School Can Replace You As a Parent

Whatever method of schooling you choose for your children — whether public or Christian — you still have the responsibility of providing them with a Christian upbringing. God has given that duty to you as a parent, and no school can do your job for you.

So many parents mistakenly think they are doing their job of spiritually teaching and training their kids by sending them to a Christian school. But this simply isn't true. Christian schools can make our job easier, but they can't do it alone.

Whatever school you choose, you must still ask yourself this important question: As a Christian parent, how involved am I willing to be to insure that my children will receive a Bible-based education?

If you send your kids to a Christian school, you share the responsibility for grounding them in God's Word. They can get an education based on the same biblical principles you are teaching them at home, so your God-given job is easier. What you teach them and what the school teaches them should complement each other. Then you won't have to be constantly un-teaching them what they are learning in school, the way you have to do with public schooling.

If you decide to send your kids to a public school, remember how they will be exposed to secular thinking. So you must assume the responsibility of grounding them in biblical principles at home. Then they can be part of the public school system without negative effects. This is an everyday commitment:

- What did my children learn in school today?

- What are they studying?

- What do their textbooks say?

- How does that compare with the biblical principles I am teaching them at home?

Many parents don't want to be that involved in their children's education, because it requires a tremendous commitment of time and energy. They don't, or won't, take the time to check their kid's homework or talk with them each day about what is going on at school and what they are learning. That's why the Christian school becomes more of a necessity. If you have checked out a Christian school closely in the beginning, you can be more confident about what your children are being taught.

Some parents also make the mistake of thinking that by sending their children to a Christian school, they won't have to deal with the influences of the world. They won't have to teach their kids about sex or drugs. They won't have to deal with the discrimination and bigotry in our world. They see the Christian school as a place where there is no contact with the outside world and their kids are "safe."

This is an illusion. No such place exists on this earth. We have to teach our children how to live in this world without being a part of it. In Christian schools, as in public schools, there are illegal drugs, sex, drinking, etc. These problems may not be as widespread or as open, but they are there just the same. We can't escape sin. It isn't just out there somewhere; it's close at hand. And God demands that we teach and train our children at home, so they will know how to deal with the world.

We can also combat the problems in our schools by getting involved. We need to know the teachers and principals. We need to attend school meetings and functions. We need to talk to other parents and students. We need to volunteer to serve on committees. Then we will find out what's going on and how we can help.

The Option of Home Schooling

For parents who want to control their children's total education, there is the option of home schooling. Today there are some fine Christian independent study programs available. But home schooling requires a tremendous commitment of time and energy on the part of the parents. And very few parents are really qualified to give their children as good an education as they could receive at a good Christian school.

Make a Choice

So what should you choose? If you are going to follow the Lord's command to raise your children in the biblical way, you can:

1. Choose a Christian school which meets your purposes and allow it to help you raise your children according to the Bible.

2. Teach your children yourself at home so that you know what they are being taught.

3. Send your children to public school and work harder to teach them biblical principles at home.

You have to decide: *What is the right choice for my children?*

Before you make your choice, think about it carefully — and pray! Ask God to give you wisdom and discernment.

Then check out the schools thoroughly and decide which one meets your needs and those of your children.

13

Know What Your Children Are Listening To, Watching and Playing With!

Computer people have a principle which says, "Garbage in, garbage out." In other words, what you put into the computer is what will come out. Jesus applied the same principle to us in Matthew when He said, **A good man out of the good treasure of the heart bringeth forth good things: and an evil man out of the evil treasure bringeth forth evil things** (Matt. 12:35).

What Jesus was saying is whatever we store up in our hearts is what comes out of us in our speech and actions. If we have good stored up, then good will come out. If we have bad stored up, then bad will come out. That's why it's so important that we know what our children are putting into themselves. As Christian parents, we need to be concerned about the kinds of music they listen to, the programs they watch on TV, and the toys they play with. If their hearts are filled with garbage, their lives will live in garbage.

Listen to the Words in Your Children's Music

If someone tried to seduce one of your kids, you would do something — and fast! But when we let our kids listen to anything and everything that comes across the airwaves today, that's exactly what is happening. Satan is trying to seduce them into sin, and he is using modern music to do it!

The wife of a former U.S. congressman tells how she bought their ten-year-old son a popular music album as a reward for a job he had done well. When she took it home, she had no idea what it contained.

Several days later as she was cleaning house, she heard the album being played in her son's room, and she couldn't believe what she heard! Thinking she must be mistaken, she went to his room and listened closely to the words. Sure enough, she had heard exactly what she thought she had — a song about masturbation!

She said it made her angry that the record industry can market such explicit sexual garbage without the consumer knowing what he's buying. She joined with other wives of political leaders to warn the public of the dangers of popular rock music and to force the music industry to clean up its act.

The group they formed wants record companies to put warning labels on sexually explicit albums or to print the lyrics on the album covers so consumers can see what they are buying before they purchase it.

Don't Be Naive

Some parents might say, "Oh, rock and roll is just a fad that kids go through. They'll outgrow it. Didn't our parents object to our music, too?" But parents who say this are naive.

One father said he never bothered to listen to the lyrics of his son's rock music because it was too loud. Well, the boogie-woogie music of our day was a far cry from today's rock music. Elvis was a gospel singer compared to the rock singers of this day.

Don't let Satan put blinders on your eyes. Some of the music we hear on radio and television today is a giant leap from the "tame" rock-and-roll music that was being played even a few years ago.

Much of today's music — hard rock, porn rock, heavy metal and rap — does nothing more than promote different forms of evil: rebellion against parents and society, illicit sex, incest, homosexuality, violence, even devil worship. Some lyrics actually recommend suicide, drugs, alcohol and even murder as ways of solving problems. Homosexual and bisexual groups boldly perform songs with explicit lyrics that support their lifestyles. Other groups perform gross sexual acts during their live performances. And all this is directed toward our kids — the rock industry's target market!

In our opinion this type of music comes directly from Satan. These groups use their music, their lyrics and their performances to encourage perversion, violence, rebellion and idolatry among the kids.

God's Word says we are to **put on the Lord Jesus Christ, and make not provision for the flesh, to fulfil the lusts thereof** (Rom. 13:14). *The New International Version* says it this way: **...clothe yourselves with the Lord Jesus Christ, and do not think about how to gratify the desires of the sinful nature.** As Christians we are not to let our minds be filled with the garbage of immorality and sin; we are to fill ourselves with Jesus Christ.

The apostle Paul told the Ephesian church:

> **...you must no longer live as the Gentiles do, in the futility of their thinking. They are darkened in their understanding and separated from the life of God because of the ignorance that is in them due to the hardening of their hearts. Having lost all sensitivity, they have given themselves over to sensuality so as to indulge in every kind of impurity, with a continual lust for more.**

> You, however, did not come to know Christ that
> way. Surely you heard of him and were taught in him
> in accordance with the truth that is in Jesus. You were
> taught, with regard to your former way of life, to put off
> your old self, which is being corrupted by its deceitful
> desires; to be made new in the attitude of your minds;
> and to put on the new self, created to be like God in
> true righteousness and holiness.
>
> Ephesians 4:17-23 NIV

We must not allow Satan to fill our children's minds
with his destructive garbage. Such music will affect their
view of how the real world operates. It can pervert their
moral thinking until they begin to believe that sex with
their brother or sister is acceptable, that suicide may be the
answer to their problems, that drugs are fun. No one can
listen to this kind of filth for weeks, months, even years,
without being affected by it.

Now Satan has discovered a new way to get his message
of destruction across to our kids. With the development of
rock music videos shown regularly on TV, he peddles his
filth through their eyes as well as their ears. Today they can
watch the rock stars acting out their perverse, immoral and
often violent lyrics. Even songs with innocent-sounding
lyrics are often accompanied by scenes of gross violence,
usually directed toward women.

Unfortunately, while the kids are watching these videos
or listening to their rock music, Mom and Dad are too busy
doing their own thing around the house. They are too
involved with their lives to pay attention to what the kids
are hearing and seeing on radio and TV.

It's true that kids do outgrow certain types of music.
And, no, all popular music isn't bad. But we are concerned
about the popular music that is bad and how it affects them
while they are young and impressionable. Their characters

are being shaped by music that's designed to confuse them, alienate them and utterly corrupt their morals.

What You As a Parent Can Do

What can you as a responsible Christian parent do to protect your children from this monstrous evil that Satan has created?

It would be impossible for you to keep them from ever hearing immoral music, because it's everywhere. But there are some things you can do to make sure they don't become victims of it.

1. Educate Yourself

Find out about popular music groups. Listen to their lyrics. Go to record stores and look at their albums. Spend some time watching them on TV and listening to their music.

Now, we aren't saying you have to expose your mind to the filth in popular music by listening to all these groups. You can get a pretty good idea of what a group is like and what they are promoting by just looking at their albums. And you will get an even better idea by watching one of their videos on TV.

2. Talk to Your Kids About Popular Music

Now, don't preach at them; just talk to them. Tell them why you disagree with some of the groups and their lyrics. Tell them why as Christians we shouldn't fill our minds with the filth of the world. Point out how some of these lyrics go against what the Bible says.

But we want to add a word of caution here. It's important when deciding what is bad for our children that we don't condemn groups and their music just because we don't like their particular style. Probably no one our age really likes most of the stuff that kids these days call music. On the other hand, not too many kids these days really appreciate the music of our day.

The important thing is that we know what the groups are saying and promoting, and whether or not it lines up with the Word of God. For instance, you shouldn't condemn your child's favorite rock group just because their rhythm is too fast and their music is too loud. What you should make a judgment on is the contents of their songs and the conduct of the group.

3. Set Limits on What Your Kids Can Watch and Listen To, at Least in Your Own Home

Of course, you can't be with your kids every minute to turn off anything offensive that might come their way over radio and TV, but you can set limits about the kind of music allowed in your home. As long as you are honest and straightforward with them about why you feel certain kinds of music are wrong, they will understand your decision not to allow that kind of music at home.

4. Provide Good Christian Music for Your Children

Young people like music, so provide them with music that builds them up in Jesus Christ. Buy albums by Christian musicians that they enjoy, and play Christian music whenever possible in your home or car. Take them to see Christian musicians whenever they come to town. Many of them share wonderful testimonies.

Again, be sure you listen to what the Christian songs are saying and find out how the singers conduct themselves. Just because a song "sounds religious" doesn't mean it lines up with the Word of God.

Instead of watching a rock music video station, encourage your family to watch Christian programs. Most cable networks have Christian stations available.

There are other things you can do to get some of this satanic garbage off the airwaves. If you hear immoral, violent or satanic lyrics on radio or TV, complain to the station. If that doesn't work, contact the Federal Communications Commission in Washington, D.C., or the record association.

You can also support groups like the National Parent-Teachers Association and the National Association of Broadcasters who are voicing concern about immoral music. Write to your representatives in Washington, D.C., and express your concern as a parent.

Television — The Other Member of Your Family

Television is an area that we definitely need to be concerned about. Whether we like it or not, TV is here to stay, and it's changing families in ways we still don't understand. It affects our family life, how we raise our kids, our beliefs and our attitudes.

In many homes, television has become a baby-sitter. With more moms working outside the home, TV has become the way to keep "latchkey" kids busy after school until one of the parents comes home from work.

When many parents get home after work, they are exhausted. So it's easier to let TV keep their kids quiet than for them to have to deal with all the problems that go along with parenting. But the temporary peace they are buying with the TV may cost them in the long run.

Children need to be active: playing, reading, running, finding out about the world around them and making new friends. Instead, they sit in front of the "idiot tube" and fill their minds with garbage. No wonder so many kids today are mixed up, overweight and out of shape.

Do You Know What They Are Watching?

Even if everything on TV were wonderful, it still isn't good for kids to sit in front of it all day long. Unfortunately, most programming is far from wonderful. Every season it seems the networks try to outdo each other with profanity, sex and violence. More and more, we are faced with sitcoms and soap operas that show us everything: extramarital affairs, parental put-downs, back-stabbing, deceit, homosexuality, incest, murder, divorce, abuse of women and abortion.

A daily diet of this kind of moral filth — for both our children and us — will eat away at the foundation of the family and all that Christianity represents. We have to first realize the powerful influence these programs are having on us and our children, and then find ways to deal with it.

Of course, the perfect solution would be for the networks to take their garbage off the air. But their attitude seems to be: "If you don't like what you see, you can turn it off." That's really a simplistic answer to the problem. As parents, we can't watch our kids every minute to protect them from the filth on TV. And it's been proven that immorality and violence on TV breeds more immorality and violence in society.

So What Can I Do?[1]

As a Christian, you have a responsibility to protect your children from the smut on the airwaves. Here are some things you as a parent can do.

1. Limit Your Family Television Viewing Time

It's important that you limit the hours your kids — and you — sit in front of the TV. Decide how many hours each week you want to give to watching TV. *Then stick to it!*

---

[1]Seymour Feshbach and Robert D. Singer, *Television and Aggression: An Experimental Field Study* (San Francisco: Jossey-Bass Inc., 1971), pp. 11-13.

To solve the problem of managing their children's viewing time, some families have simply gotten rid of their TV sets. That takes a lot of courage and determination. But these families probably have much more family togetherness than most people, and they probably know one another better.

Still, throwing out the TV is like throwing out the baby with the bath water. The TV isn't necessarily the problem. The problem is whether we control the TV or let it control us.

It's possible for you to keep your TV without being controlled by it. That, too, takes courage and determination. When you are in the habit of having the TV on continually, you will have to work hard at turning it off and finding alternative things for your family to do. But you *can* do it!

2. At the Beginning of Each Week, Decide What Your Family Is Going To Watch That Week

Part of the reason you watch so much TV is because it's so handy. You have a few minutes, so you turn on the set just to see what's on. And before you know it, hours have passed!

But you should, in advance, pick what you are going to watch and leave the TV set off the rest of the time. Then you will have much better control over your viewing time.

At the beginning of the week, sit down with your family and go over the TV listings. Pick out the programs you want to watch and circle them. Maybe each family member can pick one show to watch with the whole family that week, or you can choose all the programs together. Whatever you decide, stick to your schedule.

You will have extra time to fill up during the week, so find other things to do like reading or playing games.

If one of your shows isn't on, *leave the TV off!*

3. Discuss What You See on TV

You need to teach your kids how to watch television. So spend time discussing what you see.

Talk about the shows on the air — why some are good and some are bad.

Talk about the commercials and how advertisers try to sell you their products.

Discuss the things you see on TV and how they are different from what goes on in real life.

Talk about the values that people on TV have and how they are in relation to your values.

Talk about the differences between real violence and the make-believe violence shown on TV. Some kids don't know the difference.

4. Make Watching TV a Family Affair

As we mentioned in an earlier chapter, it's not a good idea to let your kids have TV sets in their rooms. You don't know what they are watching or how much.

To make watching TV a positive experience for your family, you should do it together. Pop some popcorn, or get out the crackers and cheese. Make it a special family time. That way, instead of TV isolating us from each other, it will bring us together.

You may say, "Does that mean I have to watch the kiddie cartoons, too?"

You may be surprised at how much you enjoy watching your children's programs. Plus, it helps you know what they are watching. And remember, it has to be a give-and-take proposition. If you want your kids to watch the educational programs you choose, you have to be willing to watch what they like.

5. Find Alternatives To Watching TV

Nowadays, most people can't imagine life without television, but there are many things you can do when TV isn't eating up your time.

Ask your kids what they would like to do. If they don't know, think of some things yourself. Play games. Read out loud. Go for a walk. Look at the stars. Go visiting. Or just talk to each other.

6. Get Involved in Changing Television Programming

If you don't like what you see on TV, do something about it. Write or call your local station and complain. Write letters to the advertisers who sponsor the programs that offend you. Advertisers listen because they want you to buy their products, and you probably won't buy the products if you are offended by the shows.

Write to the networks and tell them what shows you find offensive and why. Experience has proven that the networks do bow to public pressure. If you don't watch their shows, they stand to lose money, so they will listen.

In the same way, when you find a program that you particularly like and see as good family entertainment, let the networks and stations know about it. They have no way of really knowing what the public likes and dislikes unless we tell them.

Join an action group that is working toward taking sex and violence off TV. There is definitely power in numbers, and your support would be appreciated.

Write to your representatives in Washington, D.C. The government needs to know that as Christians we are concerned about the current state of our country's television programming and want some changes made.

You may feel that there is no point in doing anything because one person's opinion doesn't really matter, but you can be sure that your voice does count. When enough Christians get concerned and involved, we can change what goes out on the airwaves. And the place to begin is with you!

What Are Your Children Playing With?

A third area we should be concerned about today is toys. Satan is constantly looking for new weapons he can use to destroy our kids. Unfortunately, he has found one in some of the toys being sold in stores.

By themselves, toys are only things that kids play with, not necessarily good or bad. But Satan has created a way for toys to become powerful influences of evil on them.

Most toys today are only a part of a vast marketing plan that includes cartoon shows on TV, clothing, books, video tapes, movies, etc. Of course, there is nothing necessarily wrong with using these things to sell toys. Most successful items are sold through some marketing plan. But today the most popular toys represent characters of violence, mysticism or occult powers.

Everywhere you look these days — on TV and in stores — you can see some very unusual beings: half-man/half-animal characters with supernatural weapons and abilities, human characters fighting mutant or supernatural beings, strange alien characters with special powers and half-crazed human characters fighting each other. It's rare to find a show where the characters don't have some kind of supernatural power or weapon.

The one thing common to all these characters is violence. They are all engaged in some kind of violence with other evil creatures. They use their supernatural powers and weapons to win over their enemies, or they use the martial arts and oriental philosophies to win.

The various toys have their own cartoon series on TV so that, each week, kids can watch their "heroes" in action. And, of course, there are always books, T-shirts and a million other things for sale with these toys' characters on them.

The danger is that young children watching these shows each week want to be like their "cartoon heroes." They want to be able to do the things they see their heroes do on TV, like fly, have supernatural powers and secret weapons, or cast magic spells. And that's where Satan makes his play. By using something as "harmless" as a cartoon show, he opens our kids' minds to accept occult powers and influences.

You may say, "But surely you don't think these toys are of the devil."

The toys may not necessarily be of the devil, but he is undoubtedly using them to capture the hearts and minds of our kids. No wonder violence and drug use today are growing among the young. Even children in elementary schools are experimenting with drugs. The rate of murder among teens and pre-teens is growing at an alarming rate. And even younger kids are involved in sex crimes, Satan worship, suicide and violence.

Parent, you have to be on guard because Satan is walking this earth **as a roaring lion...seeking whom he may devour** (1 Peter 5:8). You have to make sure his next victims aren't your kids.

So what can you do? Get involved. Find out what your children are watching. Don't assume that, just because it's a cartoon show, it's okay. See what is coming into your home through your TV set, and see if it matches up with the Word of God. If not, turn it off!

If you feel a cartoon show promotes violence and evil, tell your kids why they aren't allowed to watch it. Then, don't buy any of the toys or other items promoted by that program. Of course, it's hard when all the other kids on your block have the latest cartoon toys and your kids want them too. But you have to be firm. Your children's souls are at stake.

Let your voice be heard. Write the networks, the toy manufacturers, the local TV stations and your representatives in Washington, D.C. Join action groups that are working to ban such cartoon shows from the air or to limit how much advertising manufacturers can do on children's programs. Get informed and involved.

You *can* make a difference — in your kids' lives and in the TV programs and music and toys that are available to them today.

Here are the addresses you can write to let your voice be heard:

- FCC Chief of Complaint
  Federal Communication Commission
  Washington, D.C. 20554

- Recording Industry Association
  888 Seventh Ave.
  New York, NY 10106

- National Association of Independent Record
  Distributors and Manufacturers
  Pen Souken, NY 08109

14

Help Your Children Deal
With Family Stress

It's a tragedy, but our society today offers training for anything and everything except two of the most important jobs in the world: how to be a Christ-like mate and how to be a Christian parent.

When it comes to marriage and raising kids, we are pretty much on our own as far as the world is concerned. The only "training" most of us get are the things we learn from our parents and the advice we get from our friends.

No wonder so many marriages are falling apart these days and so many families are hurting. When we face problems in life that affect our families, many of us don't know where to turn. And Christian families today are in as much trouble as non-Christian families.

When we Christians have family problems, most of us don't feel that we can go to our churches for help. Even though the family of God is the place we are supposed to go with problems, many churches fail to help families learn to survive and thrive. We keep our problems to ourselves because we don't want our pastor or the church members to know about our troubles.

For some churches, divorce is a dirty word and counseling is only for the weak, so families with problems had better keep them to themselves. Too many pastors don't have the time, energy or training to deal with the kinds of problems families have today. And they don't know where to send those families for help.

But the Bible says, **Bear ye one another's burdens, and so fulfil the law of Christ** (Gal. 6:2). Over and over again, the New Testament tells us to pray for one another, to care for one another and to help one another. When families are in trouble, the Church should be the first line of defense.

Fortunately, God's Word is there to help us. He knows what we go through. He knows how hard it is for two people to live together as husband and wife. He knows how difficult it is to raise God-fearing children in a sinful world. That's why He put so much in His Word about families and the problems they face.

You *Can* Teach an Old Dog New Tricks

You can be sure of one thing: if you are married and have children, you will have problems. But having problems isn't a sign of spiritual weakness or failure. If it were, everyone on earth would be a failure, because everyone has problems. But some people seem to handle their problems better than others. Their children don't seem to be as affected as other children going through the same kind of thing.

Why is it that the same problem will cause one couple to split up while another couple grows closer together? Why do some kids turn to alcohol, drugs or sex when their families get into trouble while others seem to handle the hurt in positive ways?

The answer is two-fold: what we are and how we act.

Now, we can't change the fact of what we are: we are all born into sin. We can't wave a magic wand and immediately become a new person. Only God through Jesus Christ can make us a new creation. But, according to

2 Corinthians 5:17, that's what happens when we accept Jesus as Lord and Savior. *The Amplified Bible* says it this way:

> **Therefore if any person is (ingrafted) in Christ, the Messiah, he is (a new creature altogether,) a new creation; the old (previous moral and spiritual condition) has passed away. Behold, the fresh and new has come!**

So, in our own way, we can't change who we are, but we *can* change how we act. We can learn how to be better husbands and wives and better parents.

As God by His Holy Spirit changes us on the inside, He gives us the power to change how we act. We don't have to be slaves to things like a bad temper or uncontrollable behavior or other negative actions. We can learn to speak and act in Christ-like ways.

Colossians 3:5-10 NIV says it this way:

> **Put to death, therefore, whatever belongs to your earthly nature: sexual immorality, impurity, lust, evil desires and greed, which is idolatry. Because of these, the wrath of God is coming. You used to walk in these ways, in the life you once lived. But now you must rid yourselves of all such things as these: anger, rage, malice, slander, and filthy language from your lips. Do not lie to each other, since you have taken off your old self with its practices and have put on the new self, which is being renewed in knowledge in the image of its Creator.**

Romans 12:2 NIV tells us, **Do not conform any longer to the pattern of this world, but be transformed by the renewing of your mind.** And how do we do this? **...we lead every thought and purpose away captive into the obedience of Christ, the Messiah, the Anointed One** (2 Cor. 10:5 AMP).

How we act is a matter of choice. We can choose to do the right thing, even if we don't feel like doing it. God's

Word tells us how we are to act and behave. It tells us what to do before and after the storms of life come. That's why we need to know God's Word thoroughly. We don't have to depend on advice from our parents and friends when a crisis comes. If we know the Word of God, we will know what to do when the problems come.

Divorce Doesn't Have To Be the End

Without doubt, one of the most devastating things a family will ever experience is divorce. In many ways it's even harder than the death of a parent, because divorce never ends. The pain and hurt it causes for both parents and children can last a lifetime.

God hates divorce because He knows how hurtful and destructive it is. Malachi 2:16 AMP says, **For the Lord, the God of Israel, says: I hate divorce....** It was never a part of His plan, never what He wanted for us. Jesus said, **...What therefore God hath joined together, let not man put asunder** (Matt. 19:6).

Yet, divorce happens even to Christians. We are still imperfect people living in a sinful world. We still make mistakes. We miss God's will. We mess up our lives. We don't live up to God's perfect plan for us. We fail.

How To Handle Divorce

So what do we do when it happens to us? How can we help our children survive in the best possible way?

1. Pray for Each Other

There is nothing so powerful as prayer. As James 5:16 says, **Confess your faults one to another, and pray one for another, that ye may be healed. The effectual fervent prayer of a righteous man availeth much.** *The Amplified Bible* translates the last sentence of this verse as: **The** earnest (heartfelt, continued) prayer of a righteous man makes tremendous power available — dynamic in its working.

Pray for your children and ask them to pray for you. Share your hurt and pain with each other. Remember, no matter how much you are suffering, your kids are hurting, too. Your world is falling apart, but so is theirs. Their dreams and desires have been shattered just like yours, and you all need the healing power of prayer.

You don't have to go into all the details of your divorce, telling your kids about the "terrible things" their mom or dad did to you. They probably know it already. What you need to tell them is that you are hurting, that you need their prayers.

When you pray, ask God to bring healing and wholeness to your family and to the situation. Pray for your former spouse that, if needed, God will save him or her, and that He will help him or her in whatever ways necessary.

Pray that God in His wisdom will bring the very best out of the situation. It may mean that at some point God will bring you and your former mate together again. Or it may mean that He will bring other people into your life. The important thing is that your children know there is hope. Things will be different, but with God there can still be joy and fulfillment in life.

2. Don't Place Blame

It really doesn't help much to blame your former spouse for all the problems. In most situations, both individuals are to blame. Even if your spouse was the cause of the problems, you know the truth — and God knows the truth. The rest is better left unsaid. Running down your former mate in front of your kids only hurts them and makes them think less of you. If they are old enough to understand the situation, they probably know what went on anyway.

Follow the old saying, "If you can't say anything nice, don't say anything at all." Commit your anger and hurt to God, and let Him deal with it. It isn't fair to put that kind of burden on your kids. After all, no matter what kind of person you think your former spouse is, he or she is still the parent of your children. No divorce will ever change that.

Don't try to get your children's sympathy and support by laying all the blame for what happened on the other parent. Kids aren't dumb. They have seen and heard things. If you realize you were responsible for some of the problems in your marriage, be man or woman enough to admit it. Ask your kids to forgive you for any mistakes you have made and to pray for you. If the opportunity comes along, you may even ask your former mate to forgive you. You will take a giant step toward your healing if you can.

Let your kids know that you made mistakes but that you aren't going to let it destroy you or them. You are going to put your head up and put the past behind you. And together with the Lord's help and their support and cooperation, you are going to begin a new life together.

3. Forgive, Forgive, Forgive!

It's the best — and hardest — thing you can do. Most children who go through divorce are angry and resentful at one or both parents for turning their world upside down, for deserting them and for destroying their feelings of security. And they feel guilty for having such terrible resentments.

The cure for anger and resentment is forgiveness. And that cure begins with you. The only way you can teach your kids to forgive is by forgiving. So forgive your ex-mate and anyone else you feel had a part in your divorce — including yourself.

Now you may say, "But you don't know what I've gone through. You don't know what he did and how much he hurt me. I can't forgive him. I just want to get even!"

There is the story of a little five-year-old boy who came home angry one day because the friend he had been playing with made fun of him. Before long he had calmed down. Then he asked his mother if he could have some cookies to eat and go back out to play with his friend. She gave him several cookies, but she told him he would have to share them with his friend. She reminded him that he must forgive those who do him wrong in order to receive God's forgiveness himself.

The little boy thought for a moment, then said reluctantly, "All right, I'll forgive him...after I DON'T give him a cookie!"

If you really want to pay back a person for how he has hurt you, then forgive him. The apostle Paul wrote:

> **Dear friends, never avenge yourselves. Leave that to God, for he has said that he will repay those who deserve it. [Don't take the law into your own hands.]**
>
> **Instead, feed your enemy if he is hungry. If he is thirsty give him something to drink and you will be "heaping coals of fire on his head."**
>
> **In other words, he will feel ashamed of himself for what he has done to you. Don't let evil get the upper hand but conquer evil by doing good.**
>
> **Romans 12:19-21 TLB**

Jesus said:

> **Ye have heard that it hath been said, Thou shalt love thy neighbour, and hate thine enemy.**

> **But I say unto you, Love your enemies, bless them that curse you, do good to them that hate you, and pray for them which despitefully use you, and persecute you;**
>
> **That ye may be the children of your Father which is in heaven....**
>
> **Matthew 5:43-45**

You aren't helping your ex-spouse when you forgive him or her — you are helping yourself and your children! An unforgiving spirit holds you in bondage, not your former spouse. Forgiveness frees you from the anger and resentment that has you bound. Only then are you capable of loving and helping your kids recover.

You can't love and hate at the same time. The Bible says, **Doth a fountain send forth at the same place sweet water and bitter?** (James 3:11). You can't have bitterness and hatred in your heart toward your ex-mate and still be able to love and forgive others.

You may say, "But I have a right to be angry. After what my ex-wife did, she doesn't deserve to be forgiven!"

Maybe that's true, but God says we have to forgive anyway, just as He forgave us. And the best way to get rid of your anger and unforgiveness is by saying to Him: "God, I give You my right to be angry. I turn it loose. Now, help me forgive."

Give your right to be angry to God. Cast your hurt on His shoulders. Let Him carry those hurt feelings for you. He can handle them. You can't — and your kids can't.

Teach your children to forgive, not hate. Hatred will eat them — and you — alive. The moment they learn how to forgive, they will be set free!

4. Find Someone You Can Talk to Honestly About the Situation

When your family splits up, you need to talk to someone you can trust — a friend, a Christian counselor or a minister. Talking helps.

Now, we don't mean you should run around telling everyone how terrible your ex-mate is. But it's okay when you privately share the situation with another Christian who can pray for you and perhaps give you guidance from God's Word.

Don't forget that your kids also need someone to turn to. They have feelings and thoughts that they need to talk about with someone. If you make yourself available, they will probably turn to you.

Children are usually confused when a divorce happens. They have heard the arguments and the accusations. They love both parents and can see both sides. So they become confused, and their minds are full of unanswered questions. They feel that somehow they are to blame and that now they will have to choose one parent over the other.

The best thing you can do is sit down and talk with them. Encourage them to talk about how they feel, and let them ask you questions. Don't wait until they hear conflicting stories from relatives and friends about what's happening. Tell them yourself. And try to be as honest as possible. If you aren't, they will find out sooner or later, and it will be more difficult for them to trust you.

Of course, you can't and shouldn't tell them everything. Share what you feel they should know in as positive a way as possible. Say something like this: "There are some things I can't talk with you about right now. They are too painful for me, and you wouldn't understand. But in time I'll tell you about them."

The important thing is that you keep the channels of communication open. Don't get so wrapped up in your own pain that you shut out your kids. They need you. So make time to talk to each other every day, not just about the divorce but about life in general. Try to let them express their feelings — even their anger and hurt at you — without reacting negatively to them. If you can't handle things that way, then you should encourage them to talk to someone else.

You may say, "Oh, but I want to shield my children from the pain of this divorce. I'm not telling them what's going on because I want to protect them."

By not talking honestly with your kids, you are actually causing them more pain than you would by telling them the truth. Children are very sensitive. They sense what is going on, and they hear things from people around them. They can get some very distorted ideas about what is happening.

It's better to tell them the truth as simply as you can. Let them know the divorce isn't their fault and that it isn't the end of the world. Things will be different, but God is still with you, and time will heal the wounds.

5. Give Your Children a Sense of Security

It's so important during this hard time that your kids feel loved and wanted. If they ever needed you, it's now. Of course, you will be tempted to send them off with Grandma or to a friend's house for a few days, so you can sort through your own feelings. But if at all possible, don't do it.

But you may say, "How can I offer my kids security now? I don't have any security myself. I'm hurt and confused. I just want to crawl off somewhere and die!"

What you are feeling is normal. But don't pack the kids off somewhere. They need you when they are hurting. And if you let them, they can be a great source of strength to you during this time.

The biggest fear most children have about divorce is: "What did I do to cause it to happen?" Many kids struggle with guilt. They somehow feel that they are to blame, that it's their fault. So they try to become perfect children, or they withdraw into themselves so that they don't cause Mom or Dad any more worry. This way of thinking isn't healthy.

You, the parent, are the only one who can really assure your kids that the divorce was not their fault and that you still love them. Explain to them that in spite of everything that has happened, nothing is ever going to change your love for them, and you will always love them and be there for them.

Another big fear children often have is that they will lose both their parents after the divorce. But you can assure them that they will always be your kids. Just be honest with them. Don't promise them things you know you can't give them.

What we are telling you to do isn't easy. But the Lord Jesus Christ will give you the strength to do it. Your children will judge how important they are to you by how you treat them during this time of stress.

If your actions give off the wrong message to your kids — that they are unimportant and not worthwhile — they will begin to feel that way about themselves. They must have your love, approval and assurance now more than ever. If they don't get it, they can develop problems they may never overcome.

6. Don't Make the Same Mistake Twice

Many divorced people are so hurt and their self-esteem is so low that the first thing they do is run out and get involved in another relationship. A lot of them get married as quickly as possible, thinking that will take care of all their problems.

That's a big mistake. God needs time to bring emotional healing to you and to your children. He needs time to change you and make you aware of things in you that need changing. If you don't give yourself time to change and grow, you will probably end up in the same kind of relationship with the same kind of person you just divorced, making the same mistakes.

By throwing yourself into another relationship too quickly, you also rob yourself and your kids of the opportunity to learn how to truly depend on God. He will be to you a husband or wife, a brother and a friend. So give yourself time for all the emotions of the divorce to pass. Then you can truly know what God is saying to you and where He is leading you.

It's also important when you do begin dating again — if you do — that you only date Christians. And never, NEVER, N-E-V-E-R marry a non-Christian, no matter how nice or wonderful that person is. God wants to protect you from hurt, and He says don't do it!

> **Do not be unequally yoked up with unbelievers — do not make mismated alliances with them, or come under a different yoke with them [inconsistent with your faith]. For what partnership have right living and right standing with God with iniquity and lawlessness? Or how can light fellowship with darkness?...Or what has a believer in common with an unbeliever?**
> **2 Corinthians 6:14,15 AMP**

There have been some fine Christian people who were divorced and then threw their morals and principles aside to search for another mate. How tragic! Not only were they hurting themselves more, they were also hurting their children.

No wonder kids get so confused. All their lives Mom and Dad told them what was right and wrong, and how important it was to obey God's Word. Then, suddenly, a crisis came and all that teaching went out the window. That ought not be.

God's Word is true and trustworthy for every crisis in life. In fact, it's during the hard times that we can really teach our kids how to trust God and obey His Word. If God's Word is true and right when everything is going great, then it's true and right when everything is going wrong.

Please don't feel that we are trying to judge or condemn you. We know how hard it is, and we want to encourage you and lift you up.

It isn't easy to trust God when everything looks bad, and when you are lonely and confused and afraid.

It isn't easy to say no to friends who want you to go out drinking and dancing with them when you are so lonely you could die.

It isn't easy to say no to that unbeliever who wants to date you when he or she seems so nice, and you feel like you really need somebody.

But God's Word says don't do it. So stay away! Trust in God to heal the hurt and fill the void.

Your kids need to see that. It will give them greater trust in you and in God. It will help them see how much you really value God's Word and the principles you live by. That's the true test of your faith — not *Is it good enough to live by when life is easy?*, but *Is it good enough to live by when everything is going wrong?*

Never Settle for Second Best

God only wants the best for you and your children. That's why He says no to divorce, and to dating and marrying unbelievers. He wants to spare you and your kids as much pain as possible. Unfortunately, when we are in the midst of the terrible pain of divorce, it's easy to forget that.

Divorce destroys your self-esteem. It makes you feel unlovely and unlovable. You feel like no one will ever love you and want you again. But those feelings will pass. The hurts will heal. And God will bring new chances for love and relationships into your life — if you will give Him time.

That's why it is so important that you never settle for second best. Don't take the easy way out; always wait for God's best. Don't jump into the first relationship that comes your way, no matter how promising or how good it makes you feel. Trust God to know what you feel and to supply what you need.

When you wait for God's best, you are giving your children a strong message for their lives. You are telling them that you want them to have God's best, to marry Christian mates and to serve God no matter what. And you are setting an example for them to follow. How can we expect our kids to do what we ourselves are unwilling to do?

Work To Prevent Divorce From Happening

Of course, the best thing we can do to help our children overcome divorce is to make sure divorce never happens. As the old saying goes, "The best offense is a good defense." So many of us wait until it's too late before we are willing to change. It's only after our mate is gone that we realize how sick our marriage was and what we could have done to prevent a divorce.

Now, we realize that some divorces can't be prevented. Even the apostle Paul said of this situation: **But if the unbelieving partner [actually] leaves, let him do so; in such [cases the remaining] brother or sister is not morally bound** (1 Cor. 7:15 AMP). When a husband or wife walks out the door, the family is torn apart. In circumstances like that, or in cases of abuse, there isn't much we can do.

But most of us can do something to make our marriage and family stronger and better. Here are some possibilities:

1. Never marry a non-Christian.

2. Let God have first place in your home. Submit yourselves to Him and to each other in love and mutual respect.

3. Pray and read the Bible together every day.

4. Make your spouse your best friend.

5. Share your hopes and dreams with each other.

6. Put your relationship with your spouse before your children and spend time together frequently, without the kids.

7. As much as possible, try to stay out of debt. If you have trouble in this area, get some financial advice from an expert.

8. Stand together in disciplining your children, and work toward common goals.

9. Fight fair, compromise and always make up.

10. Be affectionate with each other in front of your children.

11. Treat each other with respect, and never put each other down.

12. Share the responsibilities of your home and family equally.

13. Go to church together and participate in the activities of your church.

14. Communicate with each other every day.

15. Never let the romance in your marriage die.

16. Love unconditionally and without limit. Say "I love you" every day and mean it.

17. Do everything you can to help your mate be the person God wants him or her to be.

18. Encourage — never discourage.

19. Thank God for your mate and your children, and never compare them to anyone else.

20. When you make a mistake, admit it and ask for forgiveness.

21. Forgive and forget. The past is gone, so keep looking toward the future.

22. When problems overwhelm you, get outside help.

23. Do all you can to glorify God through your marriage and your life.

24. Ask God by His Holy Spirit to give you the strength to be the person He wants you to be. He doesn't expect you to be perfect. His Word to you today is the same one He gave to the apostle Paul: **My grace is sufficient for thee: for my strength is made perfect in weakness** (2 Cor. 12:9).

You should become the person God wants you to be. But, remember, that's a lifelong job, a minute-by-minute task. It's hard sometimes to love and forgive and forget, but with God's help you can do it.

Stay True to God

Of course, there are all kinds of situations, besides divorce, that families must face today. We could spend hundreds of pages trying to tell you how to deal with each one. But instead of doing that, we just want to share with you what we feel is the most important thing you can do to weather the storms: *stay true to God*.

By this we mean several things: never give up praying, reading your Bible and going to church. Never give up trusting and believing in the Lord. Never give up expecting God's best.

Maybe your spouse has walked out on you. Maybe your kids have turned away from God. Maybe your life has fallen in shambles around you. Life can be unpredictable and cruel, but God never promised it would always be easy for His children. He did promise, however, that He would never leave you nor forsake you. He promised that He would give you His Holy Spirit to comfort and lead you. *With God in your life, there is always help and hope.*

Did those words sink in?

Read it again: *with God in your life, there is always help and hope.*

He can turn your life around.

He can turn your spouse's life around.

He can get your kids off of drugs and back into church where they belong.

He can restore your home and make it stronger than it was before.

But, remember, you have to stay true to Him!

When the pain seems too great and the storms of life too terrible, throw yourself on the love of God. You may not feel His presence. You may not know which way to turn or what to do. Just commit yourself to God, **casting all your care upon him; for he careth for you** (1 Peter 5:7).

You have to believe that the storm will pass and the pain will ease. Yes, the circumstances will change. But one thing will never change: God's love and care for you.

> **And we have known and believed the love that God hath to us. God is love; and he that dwelleth in love dwelleth in God, and God in him.**
>
> **Herein is our love made perfect, that we may have boldness in the day of judgment: because as he is, so are we in this world.**
>
> **1 John 4:16,17**

15

Children Do Grow Up!

When you are raising children, time seems to stand still. You think there is no end in sight, and your kids will never grow up.

A mother once said, "I'll be glad when my kids are grown and out from under my feet. Maybe then I'll have some peace!"

Little does that mother know. The time will come when her kids leave home, get married and become consumed with their own families and activities. But she will never be carefree. Her children will always be on her heart.

That's how God created parents. You don't control your kids after they are grown, but you forever follow them with your love, prayers and concern.

The following little essay describes the bittersweet "peace" a mother, like the one we just mentioned, was looking for:

"Someday Children Do Grow Up"

The baby is teething. The children are fighting. Your husband called and said, "Eat dinner without me."

One of these days you'll explode and shout to the kids, "Why don't you grow up and act your age?" And they will.

Or, "You guys get outside and find yourselves something to do. And don't slam the door!" And they don't.

You'll straighten their bedrooms all neat and tidy, toys displayed on the shelves, hangers in the closets, animals caged. You'll yell, "Now I want it to stay this way!" And it will.

You'll prepare a perfect dinner with a salad that hasn't had all the olives picked out and a cake with no finger traces in the icing, and you'll say, "Now THIS is a meal for company." And you'll eat it alone.

You'll yell, "I want complete privacy on the phone. No screaming. Do you hear me?" And no one will answer.

No more plastic tablecloths stained with spaghetti. No more dandelion bouquets. No more iron-on patches. No more wet, knotted shoelaces, muddy boots or rubber bands for ponytails.

Imagine, no baby-sitter for New Year's Eve, washing clothes only once a week, no PTA meetings or silly school plays where your child is a tree. No car pools, blaring stereos or forgotten lunch money.

No more Christmas presents made of paste and toothpicks. No more wet oatmeal kisses. No more tooth fairy. No more giggles in the dark, scraped knees to kiss or sticky fingers to clean. ONLY a voice asking, "Why don't you grow up?"

And the silence echoes, "I did."

—Author Unknown

Children grow up all too quickly. So make the most of the time you have with your kids and build your house on a solid foundation. This is the most important thing you can do for your family.

Now, by the words *build your house*, we don't mean the three-bedroom house where you live. We are talking about the lives of your children. For you to be able to live through the storms of adversity that will inevitably come, your home has to be built upon a solid foundation.

Jesus said that if you do this, you will be a wise person. That means anyone who doesn't do it must be a fool, and no one wants to be a fool. He said:

> **Therefore whosoever heareth these sayings of mine, and doeth them, I will liken him unto a wise man, which built his house upon a rock:**
>
> **And the rain descended, and the floods came, and the winds blew, and beat upon that house; and it fell not: for it was founded upon a rock.**
>
> **And every one that heareth these sayings of mine, and doeth them not, shall be likened unto a foolish man, which built his house upon the sand:**
>
> **And the rain descended, and the floods came, and the winds blew, and beat upon that house; and it fell: and great was the fall of it.**
>
> **Matthew 7:24-27**

You are either building your house on a rock or on sand. If you are building on sand, your home will crumble when the storms of life come. But if you are building on a rock — the Rock, Jesus Christ — your family will be able to come through those turbulent times unharmed.

Oh, you will feel the rain beating against the roof. The winds will buffet you. And the walls may even shake a little. But your family will come through the storm victorious because of the foundation you laid.

Jesus Is Your Foundation

Jesus is the foundation you need. He is your Rock of Gibraltar. Your home must be built on Him.

Now, we aren't talking about "religion," about shaking a preacher's hand or joining a church. These are good things to do, but in themselves they won't save you when trouble comes. You have to build your house on Jesus Christ and His Word. You have to have a personal relationship with Him.

Just because you are a Christian doesn't mean you won't run into storms. It doesn't guarantee that you won't be faced with troubles. But if your house has a solid foundation, God says you won't go under.

Remember the story about the disciples getting caught in a storm on the Sea of Galilee? (Luke 8:22-25.) They were out there in the middle of the lake because they were obeying Jesus. He told them to go across the lake, even though He knew a storm was coming. They got into trouble not because they were doing anything wrong but because they were following Jesus' command. When He got into the boat with His disciples, He said to them, **Let us go over unto the other side of the lake** (v. 22).

You are going to run into some tough times, too. So get ready for it. That's life. And sometimes trouble comes, even though you are doing all the right things. Psalm 34:19 says, **Many are the afflictions of the righteous....** However, the end of the verse says, **but the Lord delivereth him out of them *all*!** So when the Lord says to you, "Let's go over," that means you are going over — you can't go under!

No matter what kind of circumstances or situation you may face, it can't keep you from making it to the other side. The gates of hell shall not prevail against you — the believing parent — when you establish your family on the solid foundation of faith in Jesus Christ. (Matt. 16:18.)

Don't Panic!

When the storm comes, remember, Jesus is with you. He was in the boat with His disciples when that storm came against them. Those waves were just about to swamp that little boat, and the disciples got scared. Even though Jesus was there with them, they panicked in the midst of the storm.

Jesus was so exhausted after preaching and healing the sick that when He got into the boat, He immediately laid down and fell asleep. He wasn't afraid because He knew He was still in control of the situation.

When the storm comes and you feel like you are about to go under, don't forget that Jesus Christ is with you. He's not going to let you fail. You are going to make it. If you have built your house on the Solid Rock — Christ Jesus — no storm can overcome you.

With tears running down her cheeks, one mother shared some of her family problems with a minister. She said: "My nine-year-old son isn't getting along with the kids on the block, and he causes trouble at school. My daughter is dating a guy I don't approve of. And on top of that, I suspect my teenage son is experimenting with drugs. He's already gotten into trouble with the law. I've tried to raise my kids right, but I don't get any help from my husband. Things are so bad I can't take it anymore! I'm about to give up!"

The minister responded to her this way: "You've been hanging on the ropes, but you haven't been counted out of the fight yet. Just be strong in the Lord and get back in the ring. Look Satan straight in the eye and tell him, 'You can't defeat me, because greater is He that's in me than he that's in the world!'" (1 John 4:4.)

When those disciples started running around their boat in a panic, they weren't thinking about Jesus being on board. They were just scared! But the Master of the storm was there all the time.

So, get your eyes off the storm and focus on Jesus. He's in the same storm that you are in today, just like He was with the disciples. And He's going to bring you to the other side with victory!

God is not up in the heavens somewhere, sitting on a cloud and twiddling His thumbs. He's with you, and He lives in you! This is the believer's source of power. He says He will never leave you nor forsake you.

Jesus Speaks Peace to the Storm

When the disciples woke Him, Jesus immediately stood up in the midst of the storm. According to Mark's Gospel, all He had to say was, **Peace, be still. And the wind ceased, and there was a great calm** (Mark 4:39).

After that, the disciples, who were full of fear, looked at one another and said, **What manner of man is this, that even the wind and the sea obey him?** (v. 41).

When the enemy comes in like a flood and attacks our families, the very first thing we do is forget the power God has given us. But He has equipped each of us with the authority to keep Satan where he belongs.

So where does he belong? Under our feet! Satan is defeated! Jesus defeated him at Calvary!

Remember that. God has given us the power we need to stand against Satan.

You Have Power

Where does this power come from? After Jesus had been raised from the dead, He told His disciples:

> **Behold, I send the promise of my Father upon you: but tarry ye in the city of Jerusalem, until ye be endued with power from on high.**
>
> Luke 24:49

They were to wait for "the promise of the Father," which was the Holy Spirit.

After witnessing Jesus' resurrection from the dead, the disciples could have run out immediately and started to proclaim the good news, "He's alive!" But Jesus was saying to them, "Don't do it yet; go get some power first." He said:

Ye shall receive power, after that the Holy Ghost is come upon you: and ye shall be witnesses unto me both in Jerusalem, and in all Judaea, and in Samaria, and unto the uttermost part of the earth.

Acts 1:8

You need to realize the power you have in Jesus Christ. The same Spirit Who raised Jesus from the dead dwells in you. That means you have power over any problem or discouragement that may come your way.

If your children aren't serving the Lord even though you brought them up to live for Him, stand by faith in their behalf. Satan may come messing around, but don't turn loose of them. Remember, God isn't finished with your kids yet. You have given them to God, and He still has His hand on them. He has promised to save you and your household, and nothing can keep Him from doing it. (Acts 16:31.)

Nothing Is Too Hard for God!

Some years ago, while a minister was holding a meeting one night in New Jersey, a little lady got up right in the middle of his sermon and started walking down the aisle.

She said to him, "Sir, I've never interrupted a preacher before, but I've got to."

With tears streaming down her face, she said, "It's now 9:30. Thirty minutes from now, my son is scheduled to die in the electric chair for a murder he didn't commit. He needs a miracle!"

This was a first for that particular minister, and his heart went out to that mother. Death row is full of folks who claim they are innocent, but he believed her, so he asked the crowd to stand. He didn't know how to pray, but when that happens, we should depend on the Holy Ghost to take over and give us the right words.

So he prayed, "Lord, get hold of the real killer and make him confess his crime."

Inside he was thinking to himself: "Shut up, dummy! That man's already been tried and convicted. You don't even know him, and you're really going out on a limb! What if it doesn't happen? You'll have to face this crowd tomorrow night!"

That's what the old flesh will say every time — "What if...?" But when the Holy Spirit is praying through you, He never makes a mistake.

The very next morning the daily newspaper printed this headline in big bold letters: MAN'S LIFE SPARED FROM ELECTRIC CHAIR.

The story quoted the district attorney: "At 9:40 p.m. last night I received a phone call from a man who said, 'You're burning the wrong man tonight.'" Then after describing details of the case, the caller said he had committed the crime and was coming in to give himself up.

Later, when asked why he had confessed, all the man could say was, "Something got ahold of me!"

Remember, nothing is too hard for God! What you see and feel doesn't cancel out the truth of God's Word, so keep praying for your children. Keep standing on God's promises for them. His truth will set them free of the bondage hindering them from serving God.

Let Jesus Carry Your Load

Take your family problems to Jesus. He said:

Come unto me, all ye that labour and are heavy laden, and I will give you rest.

Take my yoke upon you, and learn of me; for I am meek and lowly in heart: and ye shall find rest unto your souls.

For my yoke is easy, and my burden is light.

Matthew 11:28-30

Jesus is saying, "Give Me your troubles; I will carry the load for you."

One morning a young boy watched as a farmer hitched up what looked like two horses together in a yoke. One was skinny, the other was heavy. The boy didn't think it was right to team those two together, so he asked, "How come you make that skinny little horse pull the same weight as the big one?"

But the farmer answered, "That little one is a mule, and he ain't pullin' nothing. The secret is in the yoke."

Then he showed the boy that while the two animals were hooked up to the same yoke, the big horse had the short end of it. So he was carrying all the weight.

He said, "When I try to get another horse to work with this one, they bite and kick at one another, and we can't get any work out of them. That old horse will only work with this mule. So I yoke them up together. The horse pulls the load, and the mule just goes along for the ride."

Jesus was saying: "Come team up with Me. I will carry the whole burden of parenting for you. All you have to do is come along for the ride. I will give you a joy that the world cannot give or take away."

As a child of God, your life is governed by His Book. The Bible is God's personal promise to you. Whatever He says, He will do.

Be wise by getting your family founded upon the Rock of God's eternal Word. The surest foundation in all the world is a personal relationship with Jesus Christ. He won't fail you — ever!

Appendix

Other Resources for Drug Prevention

- National Clearinghouse for Drug Abuse Information (NCDAI)
  P. O. Box 416
  Kensington, MD 20795

  Available pamphlets include:

  Channel One: A Government/Private Sector Partnership for Drug Abuse Prevention

  Drug Abuse Prevention for Low-Income Communities: Manual for Program Planning

  Prevention Planning Workbooks (Vols. I and II)

  Parents, Peers, and Pot II: Parents in Action

  Parents: What You Can Do About Drug Abuse

  For Parents Only

  Adolescent Peer Pressure — Theory, Correlates, and Program Implications for Drug Abuse Prevention

  Peer Pressure: It's O.K. to Say No

  Saying No: Drug Abuse Prevention Ideas for the Classroom

  Communities: What You Can Do About Drug and Alcohol Abuse

- National Clearinghouse for Alcohol Information (NCALI)
  P. O. Box 2345
  Rockville, MD 20852

  Available pamphlets include:

  > Prevention Plus: Involving Schools, Parents, and Community in Alcohol and Drug Education

  > A Guidebook for Planning Alcohol Prevention Programs With Black Youth

  > Is Beer a Four Letter Word?

  > On the Sidelines: An Adult Leader Guide for Youth Alcohol Programs

  > Alcohol Health and Research World, Summer 1982

- Superintendent of Documents
  Government Printing Office
  Washington, D.C. 20402

  > Parents, Peers, and Pot (NS 017-024-00941-5)

- Public Affairs Staff
  Drug Enforcement Administration
  Fourteenth and Eye Streets N.W.
  Washington, D.C. 20537

  > School Drug Abuse Policy Guidelines

- The National Institute on Drug Abuse
  Prevention Branch, Room 11A-33
  5600 Fishers Lane
  Rockville, MD 20857

- The National Institute on Alcohol Abuse and Alcoholism (NIAAA)
  Prevention Branch, Room 16C-14
  5600 Fishers Lane
  Rockville, MD 20857

- Every state has an ACTION agency that is responsible for volunteer activities. To locate the telephone number and address for your state ACTION office, either contact your state capitol or contact:

  ACTION
  806 Connecticut Ave., N.W.
  Washington, D.C. 20525

- For more information on the Federal Narcotics and Dangerous Drug Laws and the DEA public information and prevention program, write or call:

  Drug Enforcement Administration
  Public Affairs Office
  1405 I St., N.W.
  Washington, D.C. 20537
  (202) 633-1469

- Every state has an official agency that is responsible for the prevention and treatment of drug and alcohol problems. To locate the telephone number and address for your state agency, either contact your state capitol or contact:

  The National Association of State Alcohol and Drug Abuse Directors
  444 N. Capitol St., N.W., Suite 530
  Washington, D.C. 20001
  (202) 738-6868

- For more information about forming parent groups, parent group networking, and drug paraphernalia issues, write or call:

  National Federation of Parents for
   Drug-Free Youth
  1820 Franwall Ave., Suite 16
  Silver Spring, MD 20901
  (301) 649-7100

- For more information on forming parent groups, parent group networking, referrals and drug information packets and newsletters, write or call:

  Parents' Resource Institute for Drug Education (PRIDE)
  Robert W. Woodruff Building
  100 Edgewood Ave., Suite 1216
  Atlanta, GA 30303
  (800) 241-9746

- For pamphlets and newsletters on drug and alcohol issues for parents, professionals and community leaders, write or call:

  Committees or Correspondence
  24 Adams St.
  Danvers, MA 01923
  (617) 774-2741

- For publications and films on marijuana, cocaine and other drugs, write or call:

  The American Council for Drug Education
  6193 Executive Blvd.
  Rockville, MD 20852
  (301) 984-5700

- For information on abstracts of current drug abuse articles, how to start a Families in Action Group, and answers to specific questions about drug abuse, call or write:

  Families in Action
  Suite 300
  3845 N. Druid Hills Rd.
  Decatur, GA 30033
  (404) 325-5799

- *Dare To Discipline*, Dr. James Dobson, Bantam Books, 1970

For a list of cassette tapes
by Buddy and Pat Harrison,
or for other information, write:

Buddy and Pat Harrison
P. O. Box 25443
Tulsa, OK 74153

*Please include your prayer requests and comments
when you write.*

Other Books by Buddy Harrison

Petitioning for the Impossible

Understanding Authority for Effective Leadership

Getting in Position to Receive

Maintaining a Spirit-Filled Life

Just Do It

Count It All Joy
Eight Keys To Victory
in Times of Temptations, Tests, and Trials
Coauthored by Van Gale

The Force of Mercy

The Gift Before and Beyond Faith
Coauthored by Michael Landsman

Other Books by Pat Harrison

Learning the Ways of the Holy Spirit

Woman, Wife, Mother

**Available from your local bookstore
or from:**

HARRISON HOUSE
P. O. Box 35035
Tulsa, OK 74153

In Canada contact:

Word Alive• P. O. Box 284
Niverville, Manitoba• CANADA ROA 1EO

The Harrison House Vision

Proclaiming the truth and the power
Of the Gospel of Jesus Christ
With excellence;

Challenging Christians to
Live victoriously,
Grow spiritually,
Know God intimately.

While in Israel, the Lord spoke to him to serve as pastor to pastors and ministers. His goal is to aid ministers in the spiritual and in the natural. Ministers around the world have received blessings through Buddy's apostolic ministry since he obeyed the vision given in Israel. Under his direction, FCF has grown to become a lighthouse for other Word and Faith churches. Today over 1,000 ministers are licensed/ordained through FCF.

Pat Harrison is a woman of God who follows after love. A frequent speaker at seminars and women's meetings, she moves in the flow of the prophet and is very sensitive to the Holy Spirit.

With wisdom and understanding, she ministers powerfully on the love of God, exhorting the Body of Christ to let God's love be perfected in them. Her desire is to lift up Jesus that all men will come to know Him.

Pat and her husband, Rev. Buddy Harrison, have traveled around the world bringing light to the dark and love to the unloved. As a couple, they have ministered to churches and organizations in three continents. Pat's simplicity in teaching God's truth refreshes and encourages people.

Pat and Buddy are the parents of three beautiful children, a son and two daughters and the proud grandparents of three.

Buddy Harrison is a man walking after love with an apostolic vision for what God is doing today. He moves in the gifts of the Spirit with sensitivity and understanding. He is Founder and President of Faith Christian Fellowship International Church, Inc. and Harrison House, Inc. in Tulsa, Oklahoma. He has authored several books.

As a small boy, Buddy was healed of paralyzing polio. More than 25 years ago, he answered the call of God on his life. He is gifted vocally and began his ministry in music and the office of helps. He became Office Manager for Kenneth E. Hagin Ministries and for several years pioneered many areas as Administrator/Office Manager.

In November, 1977, the Lord instructed Buddy to start a family church, a Bible teaching center and a world outreach in Tulsa, Oklahoma. He has obeyed the Spirit of God whatever the cost. Through his obedience, Faith Christian Fellowship was born with 165 people in January, 1978. Now there are more than 400 FCF churches worldwide.

Buddy and his wife, Pat, are known around the world for their anointed teachings from the Word of God, and for their ability to communicate principles from the Word with a New Testament love. Buddy attributes any success he has to obeying the Spirit of God and living the Word.

> Marijuana Today
> Keep Off the Grass
> Twelve Is Too Old

- Committees of Correspondence, Inc.
  Box 232
  Topsfield, ME 01983

  > Quarterly Drug Abuse Newsletter

- Narcotics Education, Inc.
  6830 Laurel St. N.W.
  Washington, D.C. 20021

- Phoenix House
  164 West 74th St.
  New York, NY 10023

- PRIDE
  100 Edgewood Ave. NE, Suite 1216
  Atlanta, GA 30303

- *Not My Kid, A Family's Guide to Kids and Drugs*
  by Beth Polson and Miller Newton, Ph.D.
  Arbor House, NY
  1984

- Health Communications, Inc.
  2119-A Hollywood Blvd.
  Hollywood, FL 33020

  > Facts About Series in 12 parts: Cocaine, Marijuana, Quaaludes, LSD, PCP, Alcohol, Tobacco, Uppers, Downers, Combinations and Solvents/Inhalants.

- Public Affairs Pamphlets
  381 Park Ave. South
  New York, NY 10016

  > Understanding and Dealing With Alcoholism (No. 580)
  >
  > Drugs — Use, Misuse, Abuse (No. 515)
  >
  > Help for the Troubled Employee (No. 611)
  >
  > How To Help the Alcoholic (No. 452)
  >
  > Teenagers and Alcohol: Patterns and Dangers (No. 612)
  >
  > The Unseen Alcoholics: The Elderly (No. 602)
  >
  > The Woman Alcoholic (No. 529)
  >
  > You and Your Alcoholic Parent (No. 506)
  >
  > Children and Drugs (No. 584)
  >
  > Women and Abuse of Prescription Drugs (No. 604)

- The *Saturday Evening Post* Society
  Health Reprints
  P. O. Box 1144
  Indianapolis, IN 46206

  > Marijuana: The Myth of Harmlessness Goes Up in Smoke
  > Putting a Match to the Marijuana Myth

- American Council on Drug Education
  6193 Executive Blvd.
  Rockville, MD 20852